Embracing Success through
Skillful Supervision

Embracing Success through
Skillful Supervision

Joy Kelshall

In this book, "he" or "his" is used in a general sense and can also refer to "she" or "her".

Copyright © Joy Kelshall 2014

All rights reserved. No part of this publication may be reproduced or transmitted in any form or by any means, electronic or mechanical, including photocopy, recording, any information storage or retrieval system, or on the internet, without permission in writing from the publishers.

ISBN: 978-976-8249-64-7

Published by: Joy Kelshall

E-mail: joykelshall@gmail.com

By the same Author:
Embracing Success Through Customer Service ISBN 978-976-8244-03-1
Embracing Success Through Time Management ISBN 978-976-8054-91-3

Design & Layout by Paria Publishing Company Limited
Cover painting by Lisa O'Connor
Printed by Lightning Source

Contents

Dedication		VI
Foreword		VII
Appreciation		VIII
Introduction		XI
Chapter 1	What is Supervision?	1
Chapter 2	The Supervisor	5
Chapter 3	The Vocation of the Supervisor	9
Chapter 4	The Functions of Management	13
Chapter 5	Getting the "Powers" to Supervise	18
Chapter 6	The Supervisor's Trials - Trail #1	23
Chapter 7	Interpersonal Relationships - Trial # 2	28
Chapter 8	Interpersonal Relationships - Trial #3	31
Chapter 9	The Role of the Supervisor/Manager in Interpersonal Relationships	34
Chapter 10	Developing Interpersonal Relationship Skills	37
Chapter 11	Communication	42
Chapter 12	Improving your Communication Skills	46
Chapter 13	Knowing your Communication Style	51
Chapter 14	Time Management	57
Chapter 15	Systems of Time Management	61
Chapter 16	"Clock Time and Real Time"	65
Chapter 17	Prioritising with the 80/20 Rule	69
Chapter 18	Delegation	73
Chapter 19	Delegation Tips	77
Chapter 20	Leadership	80
Chapter 21	Leadership versus Management	84
Chapter 22	Leadership Models	88
Chapter 23	Motivation and Support	92
Chapter 24	"A Theory of Human Motivation"	95
Chapter 25	David McClelland's Human Motivation Theory	99
Chapter 26	"Know Thyself"	103
Chapter 27	Conclusion	108

Dedication

This book is dedicated to the cherished memories of my mother in law, Eileen Isabel Ayers (1918–1998) and her son, my brother in law, Andrew (Drew) Meade Kelshall (1947–2014).

Eileen's quiet gentleness was her greatest strength.
"Let us be grateful to people who make us happy; they are the charming gardeners who make our souls blossom".
- Marcel Proust

Andrew had an outgoing personality and wonderful people skills.
"Everybody loved Drew". - Roger Packer

Foreword

Everyone wants to get value for money, after all, "price is what you pay, value is what you get" (Warren Buffett), but how to do so is another matter.

One area that stands out is that the better we supervise, whether in the home or work life, the more likely we will be able to get better value for money.

As such we need to focus on improving our supervisory skills as we are all supervisors in one way or another.

This book, "Embracing Success through Skillful Supervision", will help you create a pathway to improving these skills and effectively guide you to a more valuable place.

It is a good place to start as it is simply and clearly written and makes the journey painless.

This third book in Joy Kelshall's "Embracing Success" series is an important one for everyone who is interested in supervisory skills development.

I thoroughly recommend this book as an important way to start not only in improving your supervisory skills but also to ensuring that you get real value for your money.

Bryan Lee Kelshall

(Attorney at Law & Notary Public)

Appreciation

It was Daniel J. Boorstin who said, *"In our world of big names, curiously, our true heroes tend to be anonymous. In this life of illusion and quasi-illusion, the person of solid virtues who can be admired for something more substantial than his well-knownness often proves to be the unsung hero: the teacher, the nurse, the mother, the honest cop, the hard worker at lonely, underpaid, unglamorous, unpublicised jobs".* I would like to add the supervisor to that list.

The role of the supervisor, who is most times the *"unsung hero"*, is also not always given the credit it deserves. Therefore I decided to write the third book in my embracing success series on supervision. I have chosen to introduce the supervisor as a *"super-hero"* in an effort to reinforce his amazing contributions to the success of an organisation.

In compiling this manuscript there are many persons I have to thank, they include:

- ▼ My wonderfully supportive husband and daughter, who are always my main sounding boards
- ▼ Cathryn Kelshall, who has given of her time generously in proofreading it
- ▼ Dominic Besson, whose creative skills, understanding and patience make him the best producer one can have
- ▼ Alice Besson, for both her gainful insight and meticulous contribution in fine-tuning this publication
- ▼ Lisa O'Connor, whose beautiful artwork introduces each chapter
- ▼ My mentor, Diana Mahabir-Wyatt, LLD hc, who has influenced me more than she will ever know

Thank you, thank you, thank you to all of you and also to my other family members, friends and colleagues who have added their encouragement and support.

My daughter, Jamie, first introduced this quote to me from Margaret Mead who said, *"Never doubt that a small group of thoughtful, committed citizens can change the world. Indeed, it is the only thing that ever has".* Similarly, I believe that the supervisor, when given the opportunity and support can successfully guide the staff to produce their best work ever and so positively alter the profitability of an organisation.

Joy Kelshall

Introduction

"The conventional definition of management is getting work done through people, but real management is developing people through work."

- Agha Hasan Abedi

If *"real management is developing people through work"* then it is logical to assume that the manager's job will be considered one of utmost importance in any organisation. Although another word for management is supervision, the supervisor is not always considered to be a manager. As a result, typically nine out of ten times, the supervisor lacks the autonomy to perform some of his supervisory/managerial functions which will allow his *"people"* to grow.

Business consultant and author, Peter Drucker said that *"So much of what we call management consists in making it difficult for people to work."* When we apply this proposition to those supervisors who are not deemed to be managers, it is no wonder that they demonstrate a *"damned if they do and damned if they don't"* attitude which really makes it *"difficult for people to work"* under their care.

If I were to divide the word supervision into two words, namely, super and vision I would immediately think of the comic book super hero, Superman. The story is told that as a baby, Superman or Kay-El plummeted to earth from the dying planet Krypton. He was found and adopted by the Kent family and grew up as Clark Kent. He had incredible super-human abilities, including x-ray vision and using these he became known as the hero, Superman, who was *"a champion for truth and justice"*. Subsequently, if I were to associate these same words, super and vision with the supervisor, it will be reasonable to deduce that this person will have enhanced insight as one of his attributes. He would therefore be able to foresee the future vision of the organisation. Consequently he could then guide others in the right direction because he would be always one step ahead. Imagine if we all referred to the supervisor as one of our super heroes, namely Superman. We will then be more than likely willing to give him the respect and credit he most certainly deserves.

Introduction

Therefore to be able to embrace success through skillful supervision, it is necessary to start by clearly identifying and characterising the supervisor. His managerial contribution must not be undermined since this will impact negatively in the grand scheme.

The purpose of this book is to define the supervisor and in so doing explore his position and responsibilities as a manager (super-hero?). In addition, we will reflect on skills he can build on to improve his interpersonal relationships, communication, time management, leadership, and motivational abilities. We will also identify some of the main challenges/problems he faces to enable us to better understand how his position plays a fundamental role in *"developing people through work."*

This book is designed to reinforce and bring to the forefront of our minds some of the different aspects of supervision. *"Ultimately supervision should be the vehicle to create dynamic growth, establish high professional standards and enhance quality and culturally competent services".* (Delano and Shah 2007) Nevertheless on numerous occasions, the supervisor tends to focus only on the definitive bottom line of *"profitability"*. For that reason, it is important for us to apply the brakes and concentrate on the other characteristics of supervision that contribute to this profit.

I have chosen to write this manuscript in a workbook format in an effort to encourage your participation and input. It creates an ideal opportunity for me, as well, to share some of my personal experiences as a supervisor during my tenure with an airline.

After reading this book you will be able to:

▼ Define the supervisor and characterise supervision

▼ Acknowledge the supervisor's responsibilities including his managerial duties

▼ Identify some of the main challenges/problems he may encounter

▼ Ascertain how he can enhance his expertise though improved:

- Interpersonal relationships
- Communication
- Time management
- Leadership
- Motivational and support skills

"We ordinary people might lack your great speed or your X-Ray vision, Superman, but never underestimate the power of the human mind. We carry the most dangerous weapon on Earth inside these thick skulls of ours."

- Mark Millar

Chapter 1

What is Supervision?

"Supervision can be a place where a living profession breathes and learns" - Hawkins and Shohet

Supervision has been defined as *"the act, process, or function of supervising".* According to the Oxford dictionary, when you supervise you, *"watch and direct the performance of a task or the work of a person".* There are also many words one can use to replace supervision. The English thesaurus (U.S.) records, *"oversee; manage; administer; control; run; direct; take charge of; organise; handle; superintend; watch and observe"* as some of these. The person who is responsible for supervision is typically called a supervisor and his job is to manage the activities of people and equipment in order to achieve specifically defined goals. Write your own definition of supervision:

Supervision is _____
_____
_____
_____
_____
_____
_____
_____
_____

Historical Background

A snapshot of how the title supervisor originated will help us to better understand his job. During the nineteenth century various charitable social agencies in Europe and North America recruited many volunteers and later employed some of them to visit and offer advice and support to mainly poor families. Their main job was to encourage families to become independent and self-sufficient by developing healthier life styles. In addition, these volunteers could at times request limited funds from their agencies which were only given if a family met the necessary criteria. The person who assigned the family cases, organised the work and took decisions on behalf of the agency was referred to as an *"overseer".*

Historically speaking *"overseers"* were also employed on southern plantations in the United States of America to keep slaves in line. An *"overseer"* in England was short for *"the overseer of the poor",* who was an official who administered poor relief like food, clothing etc. to impoverished people.

It was customary then that an overseer ensured that work was done well and to standard. But as these organisations grew the demand for more paid workers also increased and therefore supervision became more of *"an identified process".* This was now necessary because not only did he have to apportion work but he also had to ensure that it was properly executed. In Latin *"super"* or *"supra"* means *"over"* or *"above"* and *"videre"* means "to see or to watch". As a result, over time, the "overseer" became known as the supervisor. It is customary now for most companies to employ supervisors.

I worked in the in-flight department of an airline for many years and on board the aircraft a supervisor was referred to as a *"Purser".* There are other names that organisations use to identify their supervisors, e.g. foreman; team leader; controller; and superintendent. How are the supervisors classified in the company you work for?

"Supervision is an opportunity to bring someone back to their own mind, to show them how good they can be".
- Nancy Kline

Chapter 2

The Supervisor

> *"To supervise people, you must either surpass them in their accomplishments or despise them."*
> - Benjamin Disraeli

The stage is set for the supervisor to work side-by-side with the general workers employed by an organisation. Acting in this role divides his job into two main parts. The first deals with his hands-on duties which relate to the working or technical skills needed for his particular job. The second is his managerial responsibilities, in that he has to supervise the activities of people and equipment in order to attain clear-cut goals. This split makes his job no easy task since it results in him having to *"serve two masters"*.

The close connection he has both with the people he supervises and the manager he reports to, places him in a vulnerable position. On one hand, he physically participates in completing the technical tasks together with the staff he manages. Consequently, the famous proverb, *"familiarity breeds contempt"* becomes an on-going concern for him. Conversely because he *"gets his hands dirty"* while performing his job, the higher-ranking managers tend to overlook his managerial functions.

I remember how challenging this role was for me when I first became a supervisor. It was standard operating procedure then for the airline to promote the cabin attendant with the most years of service, to the supervisory position called a *"Purser"*. If the senior declined it, it was then offered to the next in line. The company, however, decided to level the playing field and change this accepted practice. Cabin crew would now be promoted based on individual performance and merit. In other words you now had to earn your *"wings"*. I applied, was successful and so was promoted. However, other unsuccessful seniors did not accept defeat graciously. They shouted from the rooftops that their service experiences would have made them better supervisors. They even tried to use the trade union to derail the new process.

It is important to understand that experience may or may not be related to length of service. It is a mistake to think that a person with one year's service in a company lacks the experience to handle a job as well as another with ten years. What matters is the quality of the experience you have acquired, not the number of years you took to acquire it. In my particular circumstances, some cabin crew members were doing the same job in In-flight over and over for years. Then I came along and did the same job but also continued to do other related jobs as well. Case in point, I volunteered to work in other branches of the company during slow periods. Even though, the other cabin crew members had many more years experience in our department than I had, I had exposure to other divisions of the airline. The company decided that I would be the preferred choice as a supervisor simply because I had a better understanding of how the various sections contributed towards the overall operation of the airline. They based their selection on exposure as opposed to repetition. Remember too that doing things by rote can limit one's creativity and stunt one's growth.

I can still recall, however, the teething pains of being accepted as a supervisor by both my co-workers and the managers. I had to continue to operate as part of the team and deal with all the challenges this brought. I also had to earn the respect from my manger at the same time.

"Supervisors serve as the keepers of the faith and the mentors of the young. Theirs is a quiet profession that combines the discipline of science with the aesthetic creativity of art. It is a curious paradox that at their best they are the least visible".
- Alonso, "The Quiet Profession"

Chapter 3

The Vocation of the Supervisor

"Any supervisor worth his salt would rather deal with people who attempt too much than with those who try too little."- Lee Iacocca

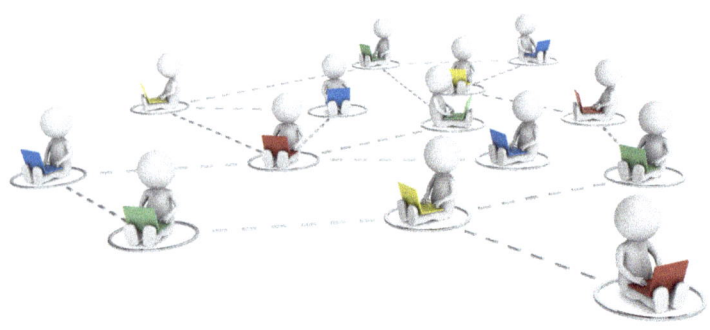

Whether it is large, small, public, private or other, an organisation will always need structure to succeed. Successful organisations rely on managers and supervisors to provide that framework and ensure that everything flows smoothly and efficiently. Even though both the managers and supervisors deal with running the operations properly, their rights, privileges and responsibilities vary. Whatever the titles, most organisational chains of command from top to bottom have the equivalent of an executive director; the senior managers; followed by middle managers; supervisors and other staff. LTG Christianson explained it simply by saying, *"We have to build the framework in which we will execute the tasks".* The supervisor is the most junior manager in this pecking order.

Managers at every level perform the tasks of planning, organising, leading and controlling. These have long been categorised as their four major functions. What differs at each level is the attention to detail given by the managers as they perform their duties. Top management takes a long term strategic focus, middle management an intermediate concentration and first-line supervisors a near term operational application

To better understand this structure and how it works, let's look at the jobs in this chain of command. The executive director/top management has to know the history of the company, recognise the competition, understand the environment as it relates to the economy of the country and know the objectives of the company. He must have vision and be able to identify future trends and requirements. Abraham Lincoln puts it in a nutshell when he said, *"If we could first know where we are and wither we are tending, we could better judge what and how to do it."* The executive director's job is to decide the direction and place the company is heading. The middle managers then work on designing the strategies and policies that must be implemented to get there. The supervisors must then put into operation these plans. They have to see the vision, understand the strategies, and then guide the team of other workers to the chosen destination. To sum up, the executive director sets the course, the managers plan the strategy and the supervisors lead the workers there.

Similar types of structures exist in most organisations. During my tenure as a supervisor, even on board the aircraft we had a chain of command. In this instance, the Captain's role would be that of the CEO. The First Officer and Flight Engineer would act as middle managers. The Purser (me) would of course be the supervisor. Then the other cabin crew will make up the general workers.

Similarly, we can even relate structure to a football team. The owner will naturally represent the CEO. The Coaches will be the middle managers. The Captain of the team will be the supervisor and the other team members will be the general workers.

The duties and responsibilities of a supervisor may vary because they are influenced by the type of organisation he is employed in. Be that as it may, there are certain common duties and responsibilities that will apply to all supervisors. We know that his job is divided into two elements—the operational and the managerial. He therefore has an obligation to support the organisation and a commitment to look after the staff. These *"two masters"* require individual attention and expertise.

The following table illustrates an overall picture of a supervisor's general duties and responsibilities to his two masters.

Organisational support	Commitment to staff
Understands his objectives; company's vision & policies	Articulates clear objectives; company's policies
Creates a safe environment to minimise danger in the work place	Maintains a safe environment to minimise risk to staff
Implements an efficient and effective operation by planning and delegating to increase production	Trains workers to do their jobs and develop their abilities and skills to improve on how they perform
Ensures quality and quantity of work	Encourages quality awareness to deliver agreed quantities
Upholds discipline and regulations	Promotes a positive work attitude, habits and teamwork
Reduces cost and expenditure	Implements safeguards and best practices in a timely manner
Establishes individual goals	Evaluates individual performances

It is clear that in satisfying these *"two masters"* the supervisor will encounter many hurdles.

"A good supervisor can step on your toes without messing up your shine." - Anonymous

Chapter 4

The Functions of Management

"Good management is the art of making problems so interesting and their solutions so constructive that everyone wants to get to work and deal with them."
- Paul Hawken

Planning, organising, leading, and controlling are the four main functions in the management process that are typical across all businesses. Think about them as phases which are designed to occur one after the other. For example a manager must first design a plan. Next he has to organise the resources needed to put his plan into action. He must then lead others to work towards implementing the relevant tasks required. Finally he has to assess the results of their work to measure the success of the plan.

If the supervisor is again likened to our super-hero Superman, his super-intelligence would enable him to create effective strategies to cope with any changes or unplanned situations that are absolutely certain to happen during these four stages. Even though the stages are meant to take place one after the other, it is more than likely that a situation may arise in any of the stages, which will have to be dealt with.

Let us go through each function to better understand the management tasks of the supervisor.

Planning: *"What do you understand planning to be?"*

_____
_____
_____
_____
_____
_____

Planning has also been defined as the process of looking ahead and setting goals, then identifying actions to achieve those goals. It also involves managing your time effectively and making work schedules. In planning, an effective tool that the supervisor can use is, the six questions in Kipling's poem:

- "What" is to be done, (goals, results, and objectives)?
- "Why" are we doing it?
- "When" will it be done?
- "Where" will it be done?
- "Who" will do it?
- "How" will it be done?

Remember a plan is a blueprint or map which will ensure that we get the results we want. Therefore you must have a clear picture of what the outcome(s) will be before you begin to organise. (With your *"super-vision"* this should be easy)

Organising follows the planning process. *"What does organising mean?"*

_____
_____
_____
_____
_____
_____

Supervisors perform this function when they divide the work into specific tasks, develop work schedules, decide where work will be performed, decide what equipment and methods will be used and delegate assignments and tasks to individuals. For example, on board the aircraft, assigning crew members to specific work positions was critical to completing our tasks in the given time restraints. Therefore, when you organise you manage resources of people, money, equipment and materials. To effectively organise you have to clearly articulate the *"what"* to your team. Each member should also know how his specific task affects the overall job as it relates to the outcome(s).

"What then does leading mean?"

_____
_____
_____
_____
_____
_____

Leading is the process of influencing other people to follow in the achievement of a common goal. The act of leading others though is not ordering them around. You are instead motivating them to work enthusiastically, intelligently and economically. Discussing, listening, demonstrating and coaching are some techniques you can use. As a leader you also have to be objective and fair. In dealing with leading others you first need to look at yourself in the mirror. Recognise your strengths and weaknesses before you look at others. You must also be willing to keep on learning how to personally improve. If you are expected to generate and sustain trust in order to develop others this most certainly begins with you. This leading function is where you have to make many decisions and the more you make, the better you get at it. Lee Iacocca said, *"Decisiveness is the one word which makes a good manager."* A good leader also makes a good manager.

"When we talk about controlling, what does it mean?"

_____
_____
_____
_____
_____

This function requires you to check how the plan is going and allows you to take the necessary action to deal with potential problems. It involves monitoring progress, delegating, assessing and evaluating tasks to ensure that the objectives are being met. It includes setting/changing the pace and keeping your team focused. Controlling also involves maintaining set standards, measuring performance against those standards, rewarding desired behaviour, and taking corrective action when necessary. Much encouragement takes place here. If there are changes to be implemented this is where it happens. It may even include scrapping the original plan and designing another. For example, if we encountered bad turbulence on a flight, we, the crew members, would have to secure the cabin and ourselves until it was safe to resume the in-flight service. Obviously with less time now to do so, we would have to make changes to it. This function of controlling clearly confirms if your goals, results and objectives are being met.

These four basic functions are ongoing, and remember, more often than not, situations arise to compromise a smooth flow. It is important therefore that the supervisor/manager stays flexible to be able to cope with any unplanned events.

"Management is, above all, a practice where art, science, and craft meet." - Henry Mintzberg

Chapter 5

Getting the "Powers" to Supervise

"How am I driving"? - Unknown

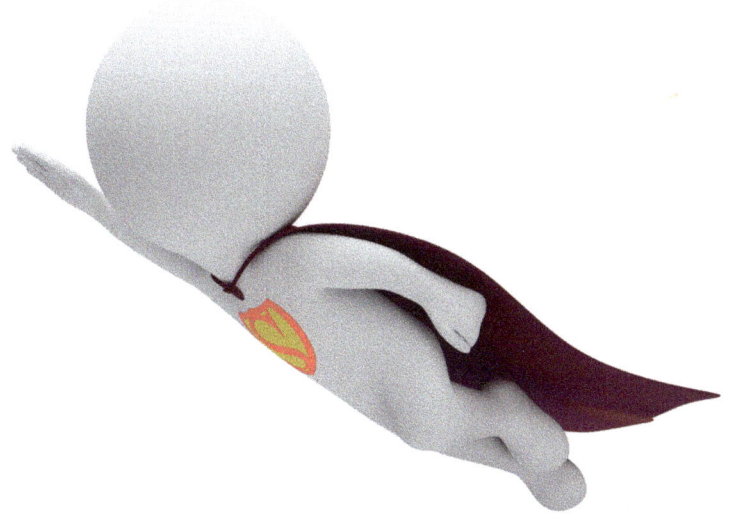

Superman's powers relied on his cells' abilities to absorb and metabolise solar energy from the sun to give him additional performance skills. So too the supervisor must receive the applicable *"power"* to supervise others. In other words he must have permission to carry out his responsibilities. His three *"power"* sources are gained by his:

1. Title
2. Talents
3. Traits

(N.B. This *"power"* can be limited by legislation, collective agreements, budget restrictions, licensing restrictions and organisational policies).

Let us examine these three sources a bit closer.

Firstly, a title *"power"* is that promotion which is given by the company or society, such as the traffic warden's arm band, the sergeant's stripes, a supervisor's white coat or pin. For me it was a purser's brooch as the symbol of the *"in-charge"* cabin crew member.

Secondly, a person may have acquired his *"power"* by virtue of his talents or expertise. It has nothing to do with his age or status. For example, on board the aircraft if a medical situation occurred, and I had a trained nurse as part of my crew I would let her control the situation. When she gave an instruction, I did as she said because she knew exactly what needed to be done.

Thirdly, one may also have authority because of his traits or personal attributes. These characteristics influence people to trust him and respect what he stands for. For example, men like Mahatma Gandhi and Martin Luther King became great leaders because of some of their personal qualities.

Which source do you think is the most important? The answer is, the supervisor should try to develop the potential authority which lies in all three areas. This is how he can go about it.

1. Title power

Regarding this first source, be certain of what your responsibilities are and the extent of your authority in relation to them. For example, a prime minister may or may not be the best politician, and will not be able to act in that position unless he was elected by the majority as prime minister. In the same way you could not act as a supervisor unless the company appointed you to act as one. When elections come around again, the prime minister could have this power taken away from him by the same process as when he was elected, by the same people, if they feel in some way that he had misused his office. In a workplace environment you too can have your position as a supervisor taken away from you if you misuse the position. You may not necessarily be fired but you can certainly be demoted. Do not exploit the authority you have been given to supervise.

2. Talents power

The second basis of authority to be developed is talents which are derived from a) experience, b) training and c) information.

   a. Experience may or may not be related to length of service. As I explained in chapter 2, it is a mistake to think that a person with one year's service in a company has necessarily less experience than one with ten years. What matters is the quality of the experience you have acquired, not the number of years you took to acquire it. Remember, the quality of experience, is exposure as opposed to repetition.

   b. Training is a continuous process needed to become a better supervisor. You need to be constantly alert to opportunities for formal training. Read, discuss, attend courses and conferences, and also ask for explanations. Learn from experienced colleagues, accept job rotation as an opportunity to learn new tasks and interact with your senior managers as often as you can to explain your position on issues. It is recommended that a supervisor have a minimum of two weeks formal training per year. Remember the reading of management books, by author Covey, for example, could be cost effective.

   c. Information is the key in the knowledge process. Be proactive and don't wait to be spoon-fed information. Find out what is going on if your own manger is too busy to update you. Ask questions if you read about a new development. If you could not attend a meeting, find out from someone who attended about the details you missed. Follow up on notices on the notice board and obtain more information if something is relevant to your department. Even if a rumour is being circulated, find out from management whether there is any truth in it. Then you can deal with it immediately, one way or another, and not bury your head in the sand.

3. Traits power

This is the third source of your authority. Whereas different leadership situations require different personal qualities, in general you need to develop your ability to:

- Get along with people
- Explain and listen
- Keep an open mind
- Know your strengths and weaknesses
- Think before you act
- Be trustworthy
- Be kind and considerate
- Empathise

It is important to continue to develop your knowledge, skills and personal qualities to enhance your ability to carry out all your responsibilities. List one area that you can begin to fine-tune in order to improve your supervisory role.

_____
_____
_____
_____

"I can't change the direction of the wind, but I can adjust my sails to always reach my destination."
― Jimmy Dean

Chapter 6

The Supervisor's Trials - Trial #1

"By three methods we may learn wisdom: First, by reflection, which is noblest; second, by imitation, which is easiest; and third by experience, which is the bitterest." - Confucius

Some of the key areas in which supervisors have some difficulty/challenges are:

▼ Interpersonal relationships
▼ Communication
▼ Time management
▼ Delegation
▼ Motivation and support
▼ Leadership

Interpersonal skills

Research has determined that the more successful supervisors are the ones who have good interpersonal skills. These skills have been also called soft skills, people skills and emotional intelligence. Even though technical skills are indeed necessary, it is the people skills which prevail.

Plato hit the nail on the head when he said, *"All learning has an emotional base".* Therefore despite the term you use to describe it, good interpersonal skills are critical to success. One can learn how to develop interpersonal skills when the challenges of getting along with people come along.

Interpersonal Relationships - Trial #1

My experience as a supervisor/purser in dealing with interpersonal relationships at work in the airline industry, brought with it three main challenges. Firstly, as if it were not enough that I had less years of company service, I was also much younger than many of my colleagues. They resented me being their manager and echoed their sentiments loud and clear to anyone who would listen. This meant that initially supervising some of these older persons brought with it an additional test.

"How do you manage your staff members who are older than you?"

_____
_____
_____
_____
_____
_____
_____
_____
_____
_____
_____
_____

Since they are older than you and have additionally been doing the job longer it is important to recognise their knowledge and skills. Ask questions and invite their opinions and *"know how"* to first of all build their confidence and put them at ease. Tell them that you will be relying on their expertise and try to avoid making changes right away if possible. It is super important to start by building rapport.

I recall dealing with a similar challenge as an experienced supervisor. I was conducting a training session for pilots and flight attendants and the training was being assessed and evaluated by an external auditor. He was there to observe and approve our mandatory safety training. Even though I had facilitated similar classes many times before I was not scheduled to do so that morning. I was therefore unprepared, since I was only advised by my manager of my role half an hour before the class started.

Taking a few very deep breaths, I welcomed the participants, introduced our visitor and faced my test head on. In less than half an hour into the session I was challenged on the operation of a piece of equipment by a *"senior"* colleague. Instead of becoming defensive, which would have been an automatic reaction, I invited him to share his knowledge and expertise with the class. He rose to the occasion and before you knew it the entire class was involved in a healthy and hearty discussion. Needless to say we passed with flying colours. The secret though is to acknowledge, praise, and give members of your team the space to do their jobs. It gets much easier as the time passes and you end up looking really good as a supervisor.

There will most certainly be sensitive issues to deal with. Manage the difficult situations immediately and privately so that everyone can get on with their jobs. Be assertive instead of aggressive and deal with any insubordination and/or lack of cooperation in a professional manner.

Remember the significance of getting everyone on board as soon as possible so that more time is spent working and less is devoted to *"putting out fires"*.

"You don't develop courage by being happy in your relationships everyday. You develop it by surviving difficult times and challenging adversity." - Epicurus

Chapter 7

Interpersonal Relationships - Trial # 2

"One of the most beautiful qualities of true friendship is to understand and to be understood."
- Lucius Annaeus Seneca

Another difficulty for me was that I had to deal with my friends and peers regarding my new status. Some of them had quite a difficult time facing up to the changes in our working relationship. This problem for me though, was the easiest of them all to control, because we already had more trusting relationships. However, it was an on-going task to preserve the professional relationships at work.

"How do you cope with your friends at work?"

_____
_____
_____
_____
_____
_____
_____
_____
_____
_____
_____
_____
_____
_____

The only way to deal with this is to behave toward them as you would anyone else at the office. The conflicting tendencies to go too easy or too hard on them do not work. A good idea is to discuss the new relationship with them and explain why your behaviour at work must exist solely on a professional level. It may take time to get it right, but eventually by being patient and understanding you will succeed.

My friends and I worked hard at safeguarding our friendships. I recall that I was especially mindful to always consider all the members of my crew before assigning positions on board the aircraft. In those days it was the accepted practice to allow the seniors their positions of choice and I complied with this arrangement. Additionally, I made a mental note to think twice before I acted on anything that could result in disharmony amongst us.

I once read an anonymous quote which said *"Friends are God's way of looking out for us",* therefore treasure your friends and show that you can be both an ally and a boss.

"The most beautiful discovery true friends make is that they can grow separately without growing apart."
– Elisabeth Foley

Chapter 8

Interpersonal Relationships - Trial #3

"Whenever you're in conflict with someone, there is one factor that can make the difference between damaging your relationship and deepening it. That factor is attitude." - James William

My third challenge involved using a measure of tact and diplomacy. In the hierarchical structure of the In-flight department there were also training supervisors who were not pursers. They conducted the mandatory safety training on the ground and checked flights from time to time to ensure compliance. They outranked the purser except during the time they worked on board the aircraft. There, some of them would disregard my position as the in-charge cabin crew member (purser) and literally try to usurp my authority.

"List some of the difficulties you have faced when dealing with other senior workers in your company. How do you manage them?"

_____
_____
_____
_____
_____
_____
_____
_____
_____
_____

It can be tough dealing with difficult people. When these folks undermine your position and seek to criticise, it makes it a whole lot more difficult. This is when your self-confidence and your professional courage take control and you simply thank them for their input and advise them that it will be considered when you make the final decision. Putting your foot down is necessary. Remember it is not what you do but also how you do it. There is no need to *"rise to the bait"* and if you behave like a professional, they will most likely respect you for doing so.

"A cardinal principle of Total Quality escapes too many managers; you cannot improve interdependent systems and processes until you progressively perfect interdependent, interpersonal relationships."

- Stephen Covey

Chapter 9

The Role of the Supervisor/Manager in Interpersonal Relationships

"Real magic in relationships means an absence of judgment in others." - Wayne Dyer

The supervisor should play the lead role in this interpersonal relationships performance. This will allow him to be flexible and modify how he deals with various individuals and changing circumstances. Each team member is unique and probably poles apart in personality. Therefore in order for all relationships to flourish, the supervisor must invest time and attention to each and every one.

I like to think of the supervisor not only as Superman but also as the captain of the ship. As the skipper he has the overall responsibility of the well-being of his crew. However, to be able to fulfill this obligation he has to:

▼ **Connect and be involved with them on a regular basis.** This could be as simple as enquiring about their welfare and whether everything is alright. He has to do this with all the members so that no one feels left out. In addition he should not only help them to plan their day, he should also orchestrate how they operate in their day to day work. I recall that before the start of any flight, a crew briefing was always done to reinforce both the safety and service aspects we needed to consider for maximum performance. This succeeded in setting the tone for the day and it helped us all to bond both professionally and socially.

▼ **Manage delicate issues by dealing with them privately with the person involved.** This will allow the said individual to realise his mistakes without being embarrassed. It is important to speak to team members directly rather than passing on messages through someone. If wrong information is inadvertently conveyed, it will create confusion which will impact negatively on relationships.

▼ **Be approachable to the team members.** A team relies on its leader and knowing that he is readily available and easy to talk to will avoid potential problems. If any trivial squabble arises among the team members, deal with it at once. One small problem ignored can become a huge setback later.

▼ **Make time to guide, motivate and support all members of the team.** Timely planned meetings can help update everyone and ensure that they are all on the same page. It is a good idea to also plan social activities to encourage friendships and goodwill. Celebrate the diverse cultural events and delegate these responsibilities to them. This will develop their confidence and encourage healthy relationships.

▼ **Show appreciation and suitably reward workers who perform well.** This encourages them to excel and deliver results every time. Guard against being too harsh on the ones that do not perform well and show them how to improve.

As the captain of the ship and the lead professional, the supervisor, by acting in this manner, will ensure that the team is functional and their work is harmonised and consistently first-class. It is, however, important to continue to work on strengthening these relationships. In the following chapter we will examine some interpersonal skills needed for relationships to succeed.

"A relationship requires a lot of work and commitment." - Greta Scacchi

Chapter 10

Developing
Interpersonal Relationship Skills

"Each relationship nurtures a strength or weakness within you." - Mike Murdock

As the supervisor you need to not only know how to connect with your colleagues, but also you should learn how to improve your interpersonal relationship skills to nurture your relationships with them. This is when trust joins the cast to play the supporting role. Your staffs need to know that they can confide and rely on you. I have used the pneumonic *"Trustworthy"* to encapsulate how you can earn this trust. I believe that trust forms the backbone of these relationships.

T - Trust - Being trustworthy helps you to gain the confidence of your fellow workers. In your supervisory position you will learn some personal details of members of your team. You are obliged to keep this information to yourself and always exercise discretion in dealing with them.

R - Respect - It is unprofessional to behave inappropriately with your colleagues. Do not shout at them or be rude to them. Value their time and show consideration for their feelings. Business etiquette requires that all employees must behave in the acceptable way at the workplace. Be polite to everyone and observe office protocol at all times. Remember that respect has nothing to do with whether you like or dislike someone.

U - Understand - Be a little more understanding and compromising to avoid unnecessary conflicts at work. Put yourself in your colleague's shoes and try to appreciate his point of view before making any important decisions. I once read this excerpt which says it all, *"When I was 5 years old, my mom always told me that happiness was the key to life. When I went to school they asked me what I wanted to become when I grew up. I wrote down, "happy". They told me I didn't understand the assignment and I told them that they didn't understand life."*

S - Support your fellow workers and make them feel special. Show how much you care for them by standing by them especially at difficult times. Lend a kind ear to their worries and offer a helping hand. Remember their birthdays, anniversaries etc. and make the effort to make them feel special. Sometimes it's the little things that matter the most.

T - Thank them if they have done something for you, the other staff or even the organisation. The good work of employees must be acknowledged and appreciated publicly. Remember to suitably compensate them also.

W - Wisdom - Exercise good judgment and be able to justify your rulings. Be unbiased and fair in all your dealings and lead by example. No one is perfect, so do not always find fault. The best advice I got in dealing with others' imperfections is to highlight something they do really well to counter balance the conversation.

O - Optimistic - Look on the bright side of things and be positive and happy. Smile, it goes a long way to put others at ease. Welcome new ideas and keep thinking outside the box. Look for new methods to explore to increase production and create revenue.

R - Restore confidence by being honest and straight-forward. If someone in your team is doing something wrong, talk to him directly about it. Guard against anyone spreading false allegations and misinformation about another. Remind them that making fun of fellow workers spoil relationships and eventually turn *"friends into foes".* If a rumor is being bandied around the office about the company's business, you must go straight to the right source to authenticate its validity. Then follow up by informing every one of your findings to repair any damage caused and put a stop to it.

T - Talk & listen - communicate As the supervisor you need to have effective communication skills (both oral as well as written) for healthy interpersonal relationships. You must be careful about the pitch and tone of your voice. Never be too loud or too soft. Being loud sometimes is considered rude and being too soft signifies lack of interest in the other person. Your choice of words is also equally important. Avoid using slang and cursing at the workplace. Listening and confirming what you heard helps to avoid misunderstandings and confusion.

H - Have patience and after listening empathise so that you understand the other person's point of view as well before jumping to conclusions. Remember too that we all learn differently and devise various methods of training.

Y - The yardstick you use to measure workers performance must be based on the company's standards and not yours or anyone else. It is okay to encourage staff to go the extra mile and beyond the call of duty but the execution of their duties must be evaluated fairly using the parameters set out by the organisation.

I read this article which hits the nail on its head regarding trust. *"A little girl and her father were crossing a bridge. The father was kind of scared so he asked his little daughter: "Sweetheart, please hold my hand so that you don't fall into the river."* The little girl said: *"No, Dad. You hold my hand." "What's the difference?"* asked the puzzled father. *"There's a big difference,"* replied the little girl. *"If I hold your hand and something happens to me, chances are that I may let your hand go. But if you hold my hand, I know for sure that no matter what happens, you will never let my hand go."* In any relationship, the essence of trust is not in its bind, but in its bond."

Relationships built on trust and seasoned with professionalism will survive the challenging and changing landscape. You will be an inspiration to others and in so doing encourage them to soar to great heights. Therefore hone your people skills. Remember whether you call it soft skills, people skills or emotional intelligence, you need them to succeed as a supervisor.

"A person isn't who they are during the last conversation you had with them - they're who they've been throughout your whole relationship."
- Rainer Maria Rilke

Chapter 11

Communication

"Assumptions are the termites of relationships."
- Henry Winkler

Communication is directly linked to and intrinsically woven into successful relationships. If *"assumptions are the termites of relationships"* then communication would have to be the nourishment needed to sustain rapport. We usually communicate by sharing information, thoughts and feelings; speaking; writing; and/or with our body language. When the content of what we express is received and understood by another in the way it was intended, this improves the interaction and is referred to as effective communication. Effective communication skills are a must if you want to be a successful supervisor. Write down your own definition of communication.

Communication _____
_____
_____
_____
_____
_____
_____
_____
_____

Other definitions are:
▼ *"The act or process of communicating; fact of being communicated"*
▼ *"The imparting or interchange of thoughts, opinions, or information by speech, writing, or signs"*

▼ *"Something imparted, interchanged, or transmitted"*
▼ *"A document or message imparting news, views, information etc."*

Understanding why we communicate will enable us to improve our skills. Nauka Shah, author of many leadership articles, wrote an editorial on four communication goals. She recorded them as:

1. *"To inform e.g. survey or outcome of product testing*
2. *To request e.g. asking for a specific action*
3. *To persuade e.g. reinforce or change one's belief about a topic*
4. *To build relationships e.g. building goodwill between you and the receiver".*

When you consider these four goals as they relate to the supervisor, it is clear that you will have to do more than get and share information. You will also have to ensure that both you and the people you manage share a mutual understanding of it. Additionally you will have to use your influence to help some people change how they behave. Therefore of all the goals you set for yourself, one of the most important deals with effective communication.

The communication process

Communication is a two-way process. It starts with your understanding of the information you want to share with someone else. You then choose how you want to reveal this, for example, whether by speech or writing. You convey your details/message to the person at the other end of the communication process who is listening and interpreting what is being disclosed. He should then verbally or in writing confirm to you what he understood the message to be to complete the communication cycle.

However, if what he heard was not what was intended by you, you will have to repeat or restate the data. The aim of this two-way process is to establish a common awareness of the message.

Two important aspects of communication lie in the clarity of the message and the listening to understand feature.

I can recall how difficult it was to communicate, on board the aircraft, with passengers who did not speak English. We really had to go back and forth with the help of sign language before we got it right.

In the next chapter we will explore how to improve our communication skills.

"Communication works for those who work at it."
- John Powell

Chapter 12

Improving your Communication Skills

"Communication - the human connection - is the key to personal and career success." - Paul J. Meyer

We have established that to effectively communicate, two people must perceive the same message. This means that the sender was clear in delivering the content and intent of the message, and the receiver listened and understood it. In communication it is important, too, that the right medium or channel is used. For example, if you send a fax and the person does not get it, have you communicated? No, you have simply sent a message.

One of the most important aspects of communication is listening since it helps to overcome most of the communication barriers. Barriers such as noise, emotions, mind clutter, lack of interest etc. can cloud the interaction.

How well do we listen? Research contends that:

"Although 50%-75% of our daily communication time is spent listening, we listen at only a 25% efficiency level.

One of the reasons we often don't listen well is because we can think faster than we can speak. Most people speak at only 125-150 words per minute. We can listen to up to 450 words per minute."

Based on that information companies have invested in formal listening skills training. They want their staff to improve their listening abilities. They know that major financial losses can occur if they don't pay heed.

One of the easiest ways to listen is to give your full attention until you have received all the data. This can be supplemented by asking questions for clarification. However, this can sometimes be easier said than done.

To improve the effectiveness of our communication, we can again, take into consideration the six questions in Rudyard Kipling's poem.

"I keep six honest serving men
(They taught me all I know)
Their names are What and Why and When
And How and Where and Who"

To paint a clearer picture let's reflect on each of the *"honest serving men".*

"What"

The message is the *"what"* in this exchange of ideas. Before you begin to converse you must have a clear understanding of what outcome(s) you want after your message is relayed. You also have to be able to clearly articulate the information. If you are unable to say what you mean then how can you expect the recipient to figure it out. Additionally, when you have to provide feedback/clarification, you should express it in terms that enable the receiver to understand it in a positive way. Focus on making it about the *"what"* and not about the other person.

"Why"

"Why" simply defines the objective and purpose of the message. As a supervisor you will benefit from explaining the *"whys"* since they provide the connecting dots in the bigger picture. The "whys" help to build rapport and they confirm better understanding. When I was a supervisor I discovered that explaining the *"whys"* made it much easier for others to grasp the importance of their contributions to reaching our goals. As a result, they worked better and smarter.

"When"

Since effective communication is a two-way process that includes listening your timing will have a major impact on the interaction. Successful listening requires giving feedback and may involve the receiver asking clarifying questions or restating what was heard to validate the intent of the message. It is annoying when you are speaking to someone and you know that he is not paying attention. Alternatively if someone wants to talk to you and you're too busy to listen, you should let them know when will be a better time for you. The timing of communication is crucial to its effectiveness, so choose the best time to get the results you want.

"How"

In delivering your message be mindful of your intonation and body language in particular. Body language includes eye contact, posture, position of hands and arms and facial expression. Body language that is inconsistent with what is being said creates a question in the mind of the listener about the real message. Effective communication dictates that both your words and body language give the same message. It is also better to choose the most appropriate medium possible to deliver the message. Sometimes putting *"pen to paper"* is more effective than a face to face encounter. Remember too, it is not what you say, but how you say it.

"Where"

Have you heard the expression that there is a *"time and place"* for everything? The *"place "* is the *"where"* in communication. Choosing the right place is essential since noise and other distractions can interfere with the conversation. It is especially important if you are dealing with a sensitive issue. If you are having trouble with someone, you have to address it privately and right away. Discuss solutions and be open to listening to what he sees as other options. It is very important therefore that the location is one which will encourage free and open dialogue and allow you both to move forward.

"Who"

You choose different words and examples when talking to children than you would when talking to an adult. So too, you should consider what words and expressions you will use to the individual members of your team. Consider the gender, intellectual abilities and the emotional state of the individual(s) to improve communication effectiveness. Emotions can negatively interfere with effective communication. For example if you are angry, your ability to send a message may be compromised. In the same way, if the receiver is upset or disagrees with the message, he may hear something quite different than what was intended by you.

Communication is one of the most powerful tools the supervisor has available. It has the ability to inspire and energise people to achieve things that they would otherwise think impossible. Many of us fail to credit effective communication with the significance it deserves and as a result our relationships fail. I believe that if you want your relationships to thrive you will have to keep sharpening your communication skills. This will not happen automatically. You will have to make a conscientious effort repeatedly to think before you speak. Not only will your relationships improve, you will also turn out to be a better supervisor. Make it your goal to sharpen your communication skills and you'll see that one of the benefits, is the strengthening of your relationships.

"The greatest communication skill is paying value to others". - Denis Waitley

Chapter 13

Knowing your Communication Style

"To effectively communicate, we must realise that we are all different in the way we perceive the world and use this understanding as a guide to our communication with others." - Anthony Robbins

There are many useful communication tools which can help the supervisor improve interactive skills. Discovering your individual style is one of them and identifying the styles of your team supports it. There are basically three established types which are called the assertive, submissive and aggressive communication styles.

Psychologist, Claire Newton, however, added two more to these three, namely the passive-aggressive, and the manipulative styles. In one of her articles she explained that we all have a typical style which we would generally use. She stated that even though we may occasionally select a particular one for a specific situation, we generally will revert to our usual way of communicating. She referred to this as our *"default"* style.

These five communication styles are identifiable by the behaviour we demonstrate and additionally by the choice of words we use. To reiterate they are namely:

▼ Assertive
▼ Aggressive
▼ Passive-aggressive
▼ Submissive
▼ Manipulative

Ms. Newton wrote, *"Being assertive means respecting yourself and other people. It is the ability to clearly express your thoughts and feelings through open, honest and direct communication".*

Obviously then an assertive communication style will be the preferred one to generally adopt, more so if you are a supervisor. Having said that, it is important to reiterate that a certain situation, for example one which threatens your safety, may demand that you choose aggressive or submissive behaviour to deal with that particular incident. An emergency situation, on board the aircraft, for example, would involve aggressive reaction from us, the crew members. We would have to shout, push, and command passengers, to get them to follow our instructions and so save their lives.

It is of interest to note that research lists the assertive style as the one least used. The good news though is that if it is not specifically your *"default"* style you can learn how to change this. Think about it, we all do individually get to choose how to behave.

To expand on the various styles:

The Assertive Style

The Oxford dictionary defines *"assertive"* as *"confident and forceful".* Characteristics of assertive behaviour include expressing your feelings, needs, ideas, and rights in ways that don't violate the rights of others. If when you act assertively you are *"honest"* and *"direct"* then this can only cultivate healthy dealings with others, including the people you supervise. I usually refer to assertiveness as simply standing up for what you believe in without *"stepping on"* others' convictions. It is all about respecting others despite the differences of their opinions, principles and values. An assertive communicator's voice and choice of words would reflect reasoning and understanding. It is certainly okay to agree to disagree.

The Aggressive Style

This style is when you choose to express how you feel at the expense of others. You stand up for your rights but ignore the rights of others. It is defensive and hostile and includes *"domination and humiliation tactics"*. The end result is that the content of the message is lost because *"behavior breeds behavior"* and the focus will be on an automatic similar reaction from others. Aggressiveness is really riding roughshod over everyone all the time. An aggressive communicator must always have the upper hand and *"win each battle"*. Shouting and bold-faced behaviours depict the aggressive style.

The Passive Aggressive Style

Ms. Newton described this style in a straightforward and uncomplicated way. She wrote it's *"a style in which people appear passive on the surface but are actually acting out their anger in indirect or behind-the-scenes ways. Prisoners of War often act in passive-aggressive ways in order to deal with an overwhelming lack of power. People who behave in this manner usually feel powerless and resentful, and express their feelings by subtly undermining the object (real or imagined) of their resentments—even if this ends up sabotaging themselves. The expression "Cut off your nose to spite your face" is a perfect description of passive-aggressive behaviour."* I could not have explained it better.

The Submissive Style

This approach stems from a feeling that others have more and important rights than you. It is all about pleasing others and avoiding disagreements and arguments. When you communicate in this manner you tend to be constantly apologising and ignoring your own rights by always giving in to what others want. This is the extreme opposite to an aggressive style. Everyone else now has your permission to ride roughshod over you. This style demonstrates a total lack of personal respect and results in low self esteem which allows others to take advantage of you. It is reflected by hesitant and timid responses from you.

The Manipulative Style

This method is *"calculating and shrewd"*. It usually camouflages the real content of what the actual message is. It influences and controls situations to its personal gains. Lying and cheating are the tools used in this technique together with capitalising on others' weaknesses. A manipulative communicator will easily fool one into believing that he has your best interest at heart. However, it is only at the end of the day that his true colours will be revealed and at that time it is too late to change the course of events. Sugar-coated expressions thrive in this style.

Understanding your own *"default"* style helps you to recognise the areas you need to improve. It also allows you to react to and deal with challenging people much more effectively. Remember anyone can learn how to become more assertive despite his *"default"* style. Ms. Newton summed it up perfectly by saying, *"If you're serious about strengthening your relationships, reducing stress from conflict and decreasing anxiety in your life, practice being more assertive. It will help you diffuse anger, reduce guilt and build better relationships both personally and professionally".*

Based on the above information ask yourself and honestly answer;

"What is my "default" style or what is my usual way of communicating?"

"How assertive am I?"

_____
_____
_____
_____

"Communication is a skill that you can learn. It's like riding a bicycle or typing. If you're willing to work at it, you can rapidly improve the quality of every part of your life." - Brian Tracy

Chapter 14

Time Management

"Time and tide wait for no man." - Geoffrey Chaucer

It is especially challenging for the supervisor to effectively manage his time. After all he is serving two masters. Remember though that as a *"superhero"* he is well equipped to confront this test and succeed.

In my book, *"Embracing Success through Time Management"*, I defined time management as *"simply a way of life"*. I used a simple analogy of planting a garden. I imagined that long before the garden can mature and the flowers bloom, will be the effort you will have put into growing them. In that, the more you invest in nurturing a healthy garden, the better the results. I believe that it is the same concept with time, the more you invest in managing yourself today, the better off you are tomorrow and in the days to come. Therefore it is essential to not only think of time management as effectively dealing with a daily series of tasks and events. You must also treat with it as an on-going, never-ending lifestyle.

I can vividly recall how challenging it was for me to manage my time, as a training officer. My job then included not only classroom activities, but also hands-on safety drills, which were conducted on board an aircraft in the hanger, or in a simulator. Coordinating both classroom training and drill exercises was quite a feat because of the time restraints they involved. In an actual emergency situation there is no time to plan how passengers will jump into the slides and get off the aircraft. The focus is more on saving lives than minor injuries. In a training session, however, the participants have the time to consider this, and we also try to avoid any injuries, so managing this exercise was easier said than done within the designated time frame.

What is time management? Write down in your own words your definition of it.

_____
_____
_____
_____
_____
_____
_____
_____

Some experts have defined time management as:

- *"A system for controlling and using time as efficiently as possible"*
- *"The ability to manage yourself within a given time"*
- *"Really a misnomer - the challenge is not to manage time, but to manage ourselves"*
- *"Managing yourself to get your specific task done in the time you allocated"*
- *"The development of a process and tools that help you be more productive and efficient"*
- *"The act or process of planning and exercising conscious control over the amount of time spent on specific activities, especially to increase effectiveness, efficiency or productivity."*

Then there is also my definition, *"Time management is simply a way of life".*

To improve your time management skills you will first have to ascertain how well you presently cope with time issues. The following self assessment is one of the simple tools to do this.

Time Management Self-Assessment

Circle *"YES"* or *"NO"* to answer the following questions.

1. Are you always on time for work? (YES / NO)
2. Are you always on time for social occasions? (YES / NO)
3. Do you complete your work and chores on time? (YES / NO)
4. Can you find everything you need quickly? (YES / NO)
5. Do you usually leave work on time? (YES / NO)
6. Do you have enough time for your family and friends? (YES / NO)
7. Do you feel in control of your life? (YES / NO)

Only when you honestly assess how well you presently handle time matters can you decide the next step. With care a garden will blossom and produce a bountiful harvest. So you too can similarly improve your time management skills and have the time to do most if not all the things you really want to do.

Remember that time once spent is gone forever and the supervisor/manger must be able to maximise the use of this important resource.

"Time is the scarcest resource of the manager; If it is not managed, nothing else can be managed."
- Peter F. Drucker

Chapter 15

Systems of Time Management

"Time is one thing that can never be retrieved. One may lose and regain friends. One may lose and regain money. Opportunity, once spurned, may come again. But the hours that are lost in idleness can never be brought back to be used in gainful pursuits"
- Winston Churchill

One of the definitions in the previous chapter for time management is *"a system for controlling and using time as efficiently as possible."* In this meaning it suggests:

The *"system"* must be created to fit a person's specific needs. One system will definitely not work for everyone.

Time is limited and always passing therefore it is hard to control it. It also will not act in isolation. Someone or something will always get in the way.

The *"system"* should be relaxed and adaptable so that it can be altered to fit changing situations.

Research has identified the evolution of four *"systems"* of time management as:

A "Things to do list" which is based on reminders. It helps you keep track of the things you want to do. For example, pick up the dry cleaning etc. The weakness of this system is that it has no real structure of timing. You do what is in front of you. You go with the flow and tend to procrastinate. If you forget to check your list you miss appointments and forget commitments.

The second system involves "planning and preparation". It uses calendars and appointment books. It is an improvement from the *"things to do lists",* however, it only sees the things on its schedule as important. Using this system results in putting schedule before people and can cause unhappiness and conflict.

The third system has "planning, prioritising and controlling". The primary style of this system is control—plan it, schedule it, manage it. Here, you increase your efficiency, strengthen your skills and give structure/ order to how you do things. In this system, however, you feel like you are *"a law unto yourself".* You want to be in control all the time forgetting that even though you can control your choices you cannot control the results of them. You also forget that you can't control people and in reality we spend much time working and living with people. Even though you become more efficient you become less effective. This system can lead to imbalance because it is too rigid and cold. If you use this system remember to always ask yourself if you are *"doing the right thing"* as opposed to *"doing things right".*

The fourth system embraces all the strengths of the above three and eliminates the weaknesses. It requires a new way of thinking and requires you to distinguish between the urgent and important. It combines whichever system you use with the "importance" factor. As a result you are able to strike a balance between your working life and your private life.

Based on this development of the systems of time management ask yourself; *"What are the important things in my personal and professional life?"* Write down three of them in order of their importance.

Personal

1.
2.
3.

Professional

1.

2.

3.

In this exercise you have identified things that really matter to you. Do you, however, spend enough time doing the important things that you have identified and if not—why not? I can recall conducting this exercise in many training groups. Often, participants included *"health"* as one of their personal choices. However, nine out of ten times, they did not exercise regularly or eat the right foods. Makes you wonder, doesn't it, of exactly how important their *"health"* is to them.

Time is a unique resource. Every day we all have the same amount which cannot be stockpiled or turned on and off or even replaced. It has to be spent at the rate of 60 seconds every minute. If the supervisor applied the importance factor in his time management, he will discover that he can actually now find the time to do things that can make a difference.

You may now have a better idea of how you spend your time. You can certainly acknowledge those important dreams and goals you want to achieve. If you use any system you are comfortable with together with the added factor of importance you are well on your way to success.

"Time is what we want most, but what we use worst." - William Penn

Chapter 16

"Clock Time and Real Time"

"Time management" is really a misnomer - the challenge is not to manage time, but to manage ourselves." - Stephen Covey

Besides the four systems or generations that research has identified, the supervisor can consider another theory to help him manage his time. I found an interesting article online written by Joe Mathews, Don Debolt and Deb Percival which introduced two types of time, namely, *"clock time and real time".*

In clock time, they believe that it encompasses all time which passes—equally. For example sixty seconds in every minute etc. However, in real time, they suggest that all time is relative. In that it flies or drags depending on what you're doing. For example, waiting in traffic can make an hour feel much longer. Whereas doing fun things just seems to make it fly. Their definition for time is *"when stuff happens".*

Here is their explanation. *"The reason time management gadgets and systems don't work is that these systems are designed to manage clock time. Clock time is irrelevant. You don't live in or even have access to clock time. You live in real time, a world in which all time flies when you are having fun or drags when you are doing your taxes. The good news is that real time is mental. It exists between your ears. You create it. Anything you create, you can manage. It's time to remove any self-sabotage or self-limitation you have around "not having enough time," or today not being "the right time" to start a business or manage your current business properly."*

They think that the three ways to spend time are *"in your thoughts, conversations and actions".* The following are some tips they recorded to help you *"master"* your time.

1. *"Carry a schedule and record all your thoughts, conversations and activities for a week.*

Useful Tip

"Clock Time and Real Time"

2. *Any activity or conversation that's important to your success should have a time assigned to it.*
3. *Plan to spend at least 50 percent of your time engaged in the thoughts, activities and conversations that produce most of your results.*
4. *Schedule time for interruptions.*
5. *Take the first 30 minutes of every day to plan your day.*
6. *Take five minutes before every call and task to decide what result you want to attain. Take five minutes after each call and activity to determine whether your desired result was achieved.*
7. *Put up a "Do not disturb" sign when you absolutely have to get work done.*
8. *Practice not answering the phone just because it's ringing and e-mails just because they show up. Disconnect instant messaging. Schedule a time to answer email and return phone calls.*
9. *Block out other distractions like Facebook and other forms of social media unless you use these tools to generate business.*
10. *Remember that it's impossible to get everything done. Also remember that odds are good that 20 percent of your thoughts, conversations and activities produce 80 percent of your results".*

Despite their stated belief that the time *"gadgets and systems"* don't work, some of their above tips correspond with some similar advice from the previous chapter's *"systems"* including how it relates to the *"importance"* factor. I believe that we are each unique and it is really all about which tool(s) work(s) for us individually. It is always a good idea to try a few theories before deciding which one is a perfect fit. Whatever label we put on time, whether clock time, real time, or generations of time, remember, at the end of the day, the *"importance"* factor is the main ingredient the supervisor must use to succeed.

The advice they gave in the tenth tip introduces Pareto's Principle or the 80/20 rule. It relates to prioritising your tasks in order to get the more important *"stuff"* done. In the next chapter we will explore this hint to clarify and give further details about what it means.

"The best thing about the future is that it comes one day at a time." - Abraham Lincoln

Chapter 17

Prioritising with the 80/20 Rule

"I learned that we can do anything, but we can't do everything... at least not at the same time. So think of your priorities not in terms of what activities you do, but when you do them. Timing is everything."

- Dan Millman

The dictionary's definition for prioritising is *"to organise according to importance"*, or *"to arrange and deal with in order of importance"*. Since time restricts the supervisor from doing everything he wants done in any particular day, he will have to decide the order of the tasks he should tackle. Prioritising these activities is the only way forward. In the previous article the 80/20 rule was introduced in tip#10.

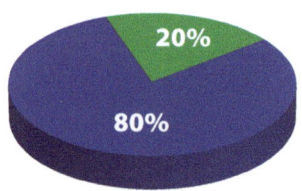

In my book on time management I explained that in setting priorities it is useful to understand the Pareto Principle which is based on the 80/20 Rule. I wrote, In 1906, an Italian economist, Vilfredo Pareto, invented a mathematical formula to illustrate the unequal distribution of wealth in his country. He explained that twenty percent of the people owned eighty percent of the wealth. In the 1940's Dr. Joseph M. Juran contended that this ratio could be applied to any scenario, with 80% representing trivial and unimportant things and the 20% symbolising the important and vital things. Even though this was not quite what Pareto intended, Dr. Juran named his conjecture the Pareto's Principle or Pareto's Law.

Despite the labelling of this 80/20 theory, we can apply this hypothesis to help us prioritise the many things we have to do on a daily basis. Simply put, if we spend 20% of our time on important activities we would get 80% results. If we spend 80% of time on trivial activities we would get only 20% results. The value of the Pareto Principle is that it allows us to focus on the 20% that really matters which will produce the 80% of results. C. Ray Johnson, in one of the final chapters of his book, CEO Logic: How to Think and Act Like a Chief Executive, summarises: *"Prioritising is the answer to time management problems—not computers, efficiency experts, or matrix scheduling. You do not need to do work faster or to eliminate gaps in productivity to make better use of your time. You need to spend more time on the right things..."*

In a nutshell, to be able to effectively prioritise you need to:

▼ Know what your objectives are.
▼ Recognise what needs to be done to meet them.
▼ Identify your strengths and weaknesses.

Only then can you move on to giving more time to the important activities and less time to the others.

Here are some examples from Billy Shall of how to use the 80/20 rule as a supervisor.

"Purge the clutter: *How many dust collector possessions do you really need? Try to donate or sell possessions that you hardly use. They are contributing to 80% of the dust.*

Reason: 80% of the space on shelves hold clutter

Improve relationships: *Focus on nurturing the small percentage of relationships that provide most value (spouse, family, close friends) Moments spent and memories made improve the quality of your relationships.*

Reason: 20% of relationships provide 80% of value

Eliminate stress: *Find the small portion of activities that produce the most stress and eliminate them.*

Reason: 20% of stressful activities produce 80% of the stress

Eliminate information overload: *Constant bombardment from news, emails, advertisements and articles are taking up time and head space. Cut down on the information consumption to the small percentage that is necessary.*

Reason: 80% of information is useless and 20% is crucial

Accomplish more in less time: *By focusing on activities that produce the most results and by eliminating or outsourcing trivial activities you can free more of your time while accomplishing more.*

Reason: 20% of activities produce 80% results"

Billy Shall also shared a personal way to use the 80/20 rule. He said:

"Lose weight: *If you cut out the small percentage of foods that contributes the most to weight gain (fatty foods, fried foods, sweets) and exercise regularly, not only will you lose weight, you'll have more energy and feel much better.*

Reason: 20% of foods contribute 80% of weight gain"

Pareto's Principle or the 80/20 Rule can assist the supervisor on a daily basis to concentrate on the 20 percent of his work that really matters, to produce the 80% results. After all, it is not only about *"working smart",* it is also about working smart on the right things. If the centre of attention is focused on your important things, you will surely be well on your way to saving time and embracing success.

"The essence of the best thinking in the area of time management can be captured in a single phrase: Organise and execute around priorities."
- Stephen Covey

Chapter 18

Delegation

"The first rule of management is delegation. Don't try and do everything yourself because you can't."
- Anthea Turner

Since it is obvious that the supervisor cannot always do everything he wants done, in addition to prioritising, delegation is another useful tool that the supervisor can employ.

Delegation has been defined as *"the process of passing certain tasks and duties from one person to another, typically a superior to a subordinate. The delegate receives sufficient authority to complete the work but the supervisor retains the overall responsibility for its success or failure."* Simply put, it is how to get work done through others. Delegation is more than just a means of distributing work among people, effective delegation also gains commitment and helps to develop your team members.

The following questions, answers and explanations are adapted from original work by Hershey and Blanchard.

Before the supervisor delegates he must be able to trust the motivation and the skills of the team members with each task being delegated. Questions he must ask himself are:

"Are they fully capable of doing the tasks?" This relates to their *"skill"* levels.

"Do they want to do the tasks?" This relates to the motivation or *"willingness"* on their part.

Depending on the answers he gets the supervisor has to then determine the appropriate level of delegation. Delegation options for him include the following:

1. If the team member is able and willing or you trust both his motivation and skills, you should give full responsibility for completing the task to him. - *"Fully delegate"* Remember when you do so, you are overall still responsible for the end results. However, this level of delegation would build his confidence and help him to grow.
2. When the team member is willing but not able or when you trust his motivation but not his skills then you should work closely with him to complete the task or assign him other developmental resources. - *"Develop"* For example, training him to develop new skills, will increase his knowledge and productivity.
3. When the team member is able but not willing or you trust his skills but not his motivation, you must monitor progress closely to ensure schedules are met. - *"Manage"* After all you know that he can do it, but because of his lack of interest, you have to help him keep his eye on the ball.
4. When the team member is neither able nor willing or you do not trust his motivation or his skills, then you should find another task to delegate. - *"Redeploy"* Some people are better suited to other tasks, or are simply, square pegs in round holes.

List some reasons why supervisors do not delegate?

_____
_____
_____
_____
_____
_____
_____
_____
_____
_____
_____
_____

Some reasons are:

▼ *"I can do the task better myself."*
▼ *"It will take too much time to explain."*
▼ *"I can do it faster."*
▼ *"I don't want to overburden my overworked staff."*
▼ *"I enjoy doing it."*
▼ *"This is too important; I can't trust anyone else to do it."*
▼ *"If I can't do it then I shouldn't ask anyone else to."*

"Nothing is impossible if you can delegate" - Unknown

Chapter 19

Delegation Tips

"You can delegate authority but you cannot delegate responsibility." - Byron Dorgan

Delegating is an important function to help supervisors manage their time more efficiently. Remember too that the opposite of delegation is micromanaging which defeats the purpose of saving time.

Why should supervisors delegate?

Supervisors should delegate because:

- ▼ It allows them to spend their personal time and energy on the tasks to which they can add the most value. It actually frees up their time to allow them to concentrate on other important matters.
- ▼ It helps to develop their staff capabilities, skills and it increases their confidence and commitment.
- ▼ It helps to build morale and team spirit and helps to motivate the staff. When work is distributed among team members it can be accomplished more efficiently.
- ▼ It allows a succession plan to form.

Bear in mind that there are tasks that you should not delegate. For example, personal requests from your boss; crisis situations and disciplinary actions should always be handled personally.

Having now chosen his approach to delegation, whether fully or otherwise, the supervisor must pay particular attention to the following to ensure positive results. The team member must:

- ▼ Have a clear understanding of what the objectives are. You must provide the big picture and explain why the task is important. *"Begin with the end in mind"* (Stephen Covey)
- ▼ Be competent, skilled and capable for the assignment.
- ▼ Be given the time, clear instructions, scope to use his initiative, resources and support.
- ▼ Be provided with a schedule or deadline expectations. Be given directions regarding what is needed and when, not how to do things
- ▼ Be treated with respect, so he doesn't feel he is just doing something you do not want to do.
- ▼ Be given feedback and praise when deserved to build on trust.

Effective delegation means that although decisions are taken lower down in the pecking order they are taken nearer to where the work is being done and problems occur. Your staff will therefore often have a much better idea of what needs to be done than you do. That means they can make decisions faster and probably better.

Therefore to delegate effectively, choose the right task, identify the right person to do it, and then do it the right way. As the supervisor when you use your time efficiently to include planning, prioritising and delegating you are really organising yourself and others. This too, reinforces the successful image of you and your staff.

"Never tell people how to do things. Tell them what to do and they will surprise you with their ingenuity."
- George S. Patton

Chapter 20

Leadership

"The key to successful leadership today is influence, not authority." - Kenneth Blanchard

Although your position as a manager or supervisor gives you the permission to organise your team to get specific tasks done, this *"power"* does not automatically make you a leader. This is because leaders are *"made and not born"*. Anyone with the aspiration and steadfast determination can become a successful leader—whether a *"good"* leader, for example, a Nelson Mandela, or a *"bad"* leader, like an Adolph Hitler. *"Good leaders develop through a never-ending process of self-study, education, training, and experience."* (Jago, 1982). Additionally, a person's personal character traits together with his knowledge and skills will also influence his ability to lead, as mentioned in a previous chapter.

What then is leadership? One definition is: *"Leadership is a process whereby an individual influences a group of individuals to achieve a common goal".* (Northouse 2007)

Identify someone who has had a huge influence in your life both personal/private and professional/work and say why this occurred?

_____
_____
_____
_____
_____

One of the persons who had an enormous influence in my professional life was a training facilitator in the airline I worked for. My introduction to the world of *"flying"* was an intensive, five week, ground training program. It included one examination after another on safety aspects; drills –theoretical and practical; equipment; aircraft; dangerous goods; and first aid to name a few. It was during this period that many participants opted to quit. The course was facilitated by a dynamic and energetic individual whose style made learning interesting and we had so much fun. I decided then and there that when I was ready to clip my wings, I would not only get involved in training but I would also try to make it as exciting as she did. It is no easy task to keep adults *"on their feet"* for five hours and she succeeded to fascinate us for five weeks.

Consequently I got involved very soon in on-the-job-training, and I helped out in the classroom as often as I could. I soon trained to become a facilitator and became an in-flight training instructor. Later on I was promoted to the manager of the in-flight department which also made me the in-flight training manager—all because of the influence of one person. It is this influence which somehow helped to mold me into the person I am today and that is what leadership is all about.

In other words, according to John Maxwell, *"leadership is influence"*. Consequently successful leaders in order to influence others will not only, like superman, have a clear vision, they will also have the ability to eloquently articulate it and as a result their followers totally *"buy into"* their concepts. Additionally they set high standards and stay true to values and beliefs. They are also able to use current events to their advantage to bond with their followers and encourage them to become *"champions for their causes".* This ability to inspire others and motivate them is the key to the leadership challenge.

"Where there is no vision the people perish."
- Proverbs 29:18

Chapter 21

Leadership versus Management

"Leadership is unlocking people's potential to become better." - Bill Bradley

Is leadership, however, the same as management?

Exercise: Answer this question below and if you do not agree, list the differences.

_____
_____
_____
_____
_____
_____
_____
_____
_____
_____
_____
_____
_____
_____
_____
_____

The following table depicts some of the answers research has identified.

Leadership vs Management

LEADERSHIP/ LEADERS	MANAGEMENT/ MANAGERS
1. He gets his *"powers"* from the trust and confidence of his followers. He provides an attainable vision for them and does not necessarily have to be a manager.	1. He gets his *"powers"* from his position in the company. Tasks get done through the efforts of others because of his status.
2. The spotlight is on people	2. The spotlight is on structure and systems
3. Develops employees, works hand in hand with them and lets them share opinions and ideas to complete tasks.	3. Copes with employees and assigns tasks to them
4. Finds solutions for problems	4. Uses policy and procedures to solve problems
5. Creates the course	5. Stays to a course
6. Listens	6. Tracks
7. Contributes to a meeting	7. Notes a meeting
8. Inspires a message	8. Delivers a message
9. Finds answers and solutions	9. Formulates the questions and identifies problems
10. Takes employees to a new place	10. Takes care of employees where you are
11. Makes decisions	11. Concerned with finding the facts
12. Focuses on effectiveness	12. Critical concern is efficiency
13. Hears when there is no sound and sees when there is no light	13. Sees and hears what is actually going on
14. Concerned with doing the right things	14. Concerned with doing the things right

Essentially a leader inspires people to not only want to be a part of his vision but also to give it their best shot. A manager, however, exercises formal authority over the activities of others to achieve company objectives. If you are able to develop your leadership potential then you can better succeed as a manager.

We know that there are unique differences between leaders and managers. It is important to acknowledge these, so as to be better able to develop the people you supervise. Additionally, to be a successful manger/supervisor, you must also be a good leader. The best way, of course, in leading is to walk your talk. Leading requires you to show your staff the way, by doing it yourself. This includes abiding by the company's rules and regulations, just like everyone else.

Additionally, it is important that you share in the vision of the organisation, and that you are able to articulate this vision to your staff members. As a supervisor, your values and beliefs must be aligned with that of the organisation. Does your organisation have values? If so, remember that it is the behaviour of all the staff members, which will demonstrate and reflect these values. Therefore, if your organisation has values like respect, and honesty, these will be manifested in how you and your staff treat with each other. It will be a positive indication that you are on the right track.

As a supervisor it is your responsibility to communicate the vision of the organisation, and ensure that the behaviour of you and your team members reflect its values. Good leadership takes a firm commitment. It simply means, doing the right things, at the right time, for the right reasons.

"A boss creates fear, a leader confidence. A boss fixes blame, a leader corrects mistakes. A boss knows all, a leader asks questions. A boss makes work drudgery, a leader makes it interesting. A boss is interested in himself or herself, a leader is interested in the group."
- Russell H. Ewin

Chapter 22

Leadership Models

"Outstanding leaders go out of their way to boost the self-esteem of their personnel. If people believe in themselves, it's amazing what they can accomplish."

- Sam Walton

There are numerous leadership models created over the years which can help you to improve your leadership capabilities. For example, Situational Leadership by Ken Blanchard and Paul Hersey; Servant Leadership by Robert K. Greenleaf; Emotional Intelligence by Daniel Coleman; Level Five Leadership by Jim Collins to name a few, all contribute to one's development. So which one is the best leadership model one can emulate?

I believe a good place to start is by adopting *"The Five Practices of Exemplary Leadership® Model"* By Jim Kouzes and Barry Posner. They are also co-authors of the award-winning, best-selling book, *"The Leadership Challenge"* They have been working together for many years to compile research and discover what all great leaders have in common. We do not have to reinvent the wheel, we can learn from their studies.

They have stated that *"leadership is not about personality, it is about behaviours".* Their results reveal the five *"behaviours"* which they believe all leaders share despite differences in background, gender or age. Leaders are at their *"personal best"* when they:

1. *"Model the Way*
2. *Inspire a shared Vision*
3. *Challenge the Process*
4. *Enable others to Act*
5. *Encourage the heart"*

To *"model the way"* leaders explain the *"whys"* and also physically show the way. They do this by *"doing as I do"* and not *"doing as I say"*. They set the bar about how they should behave to honour their values and principles. When you *"model the way"* as the supervisor, your behaviour will reflect the values of the organisation.

Leaders totally and absolutely believe in their visions. Therefore they can effortlessly convince others to join their cause and so *"inspire a shared vision".* People get excited and want to be a part of this future. As a supervisor with super-vision, this should be easy to do.

They do not accept that things must remain as they are so leaders *"challenge the process".* They are keen to explore new methods and venture into the unknown. Continuous improvement and knowledge sustain their drive and determination. Remember, you do not have to do things by rote. New technology now demands new approaches in tackling tasks.

Leaders allow the other members of the team to sometimes lead and take responsibility for tasks. To *"enable others to act"*, they respect their followers' opinions and ideas and involve them in decision making processes. It is okay to lead from behind sometimes. It helps your staff to develop new skills and become better leaders.

Finally to *"encourage the heart"* leaders recognise the contributions of the members of the team. They allow them to bask in the glory of successes. Everyone likes to be praised for their input. Both the good feeling of a job well done, and the bonus in sharing the rewards, kindle the fires in their followers' hearts and minds. Celebrating their successes encourages them to continue the good work.

The above model can help the supervisor become a strong and reliable leader. If leaders are *"made and not born"* you too, can develop your skills to be better able to inspire, and motivate your team. In a nutshell, remember it is simply leading by example and cutting your team enough slack to use their skills and initiatives to get the job done. Recognising their input and rewarding them for it becomes the icing on the cake. Your team will flourish and continue to soar to new heights of success. You will in turn look good as their leader/manager.

"A genuine leader is not a searcher for consensus but a moulder of consensus." - Martin Luther King, Jr.

Chapter 23

Motivation and Support

"Without inspiration the best powers of the mind remain dormant. There is fuel in us which needs to be ignited with sparks."
- Johann Gottfried Von Herder

The dictionary defines *"motivate"* as, *"to stimulate someone's interest in something"* or *"provide someone with a motive for doing something"*. Motivation is an important responsibility of the supervisor since it highly influences the morale of the people being supervised. It falls within the function of leading and is actually the key element in leadership.

"What are the things that motivate you as an individual at work?"

_____
_____
_____
_____

Kaizen Consulting Limited undertook research to try and understand more about what motivates people at work. The top ten most common responses were:

▼ Achievement
▼ Working with others
▼ Recognition
▼ Helping others
▼ Varied & interesting work
▼ Financial reward
▼ Good working atmosphere
▼ Empowerment
▼ Solving problems
▼ Physical environment

On the other hand, it is equally important to identify de-motivators, some of which are:

- ▼ Micromanagement
- ▼ Hazy job profile
- ▼ Politics
- ▼ No recognition
- ▼ Unrealistic workload
- ▼ Salary
- ▼ Timings
- ▼ Environment
- ▼ Policies
- ▼ Distance

As a supervisor you have to remember that motivation is not only about making people want to work for and with you, they must also benefit from doing so. I remember an incident when one of my training officers wanted to initiate a new training intervention. This required exploring unchartered waters. As the training manager, I recognised that to be able to continue to successfully motivate him, I needed to approve it. However, before giving him free rein we, the team, played devil's advocate to help him prepare for real time in the classroom. It was successful, and I was very careful to ensure that he got the credit for it.

Bottom line —even though you can get people to work well they have to see some form of personal rewards. It's the WIIFM radio station—"*What's In It For Me.*"

Maslow's hierarchy of needs, in the following chapter, is a motivational theory in psychology, which can help us better understand how to motivate others.

"Motivation is the act of getting people to do what you want them to do because they want to do it."
- Dwight Eisenhower

Chapter 24

"A Theory of Human Motivation"

"The motivation is in my heart to work towards my goals and dreams." - Nonito Donaire

In 1943 Abraham Maslow devised a theory, called *"A Theory of Human Motivation".* This theory is otherwise referred to as his pyramid, or hierarchy of needs. It suggests that basically, people will always want more than what they already have. He split these wants into five ascending levels. These levels are;

1. Physiological needs
2. Safety needs
3. Needs of belonging
4. Self-esteem
5. Self-actualisation.

Maslow's levels suggest that we can only move up to a higher level if our needs at the lower levels have been met.

In other words, we start at level one needing air to breathe, food to eat, clothes to wear etc. Having satisfied those needs we now want more and so we move up to level two. We now want not only a home to own, but also a protected environment to live in. Then we climb another level to one which provides friends, and neighbours, to fulfil our sense of belonging to an accepting society. To satisfy our ego or self-esteem needs, we then go to the next level. Here we strive for personal recognition of what we contribute to that society, with our talents and skills. The final level we try to attain, will complete us by taking us to that place where we feel truly fulfilled, and includes satisfying our spiritual needs. Maslow contends though, that in this highest level, we are all individually different with regard to what totally fulfils us.

In a working environment the levels would represent different needs. We will begin at level one with simply wanting a job. After we can collect a salary we move up to level two where we will want for example, a pension plan, health plan and job security with fair working conditions. We then want to be accepted by our colleagues as part of a team, so we climb to the belonging need level. Here we even get involved in family day activities and it is important to be liked and respected by our peers. Having accomplished this we want to be recognised for our personal contribution and so we go to the esteem need level. We strive for becoming *"employee of the month"* or similar recognition as awards for our particular skills. Finally we want to be promoted to positions where we can call the shots. Here at this final self-actualisation level we may also want to improve our skills and look for new avenues to explore.

Therefore according to Maslow if we were to adapt this theory to a work situation and try to recognise the different levels our staff members are at, we will be better able to motivate them.

Even though Maslow's theory can help us to interpret our team's needs and so motivate them other research doesn't seem to totally support his view that individuals' needs change in the order he stated. For instance, in his book, *"Understanding Organisations"* Charles Handy argues that this pyramid or hierarchy is not as fixed as Maslow contends. Handy maintains that as humans we have many needs which at any time can form a hierarchy. This hierarchy, however, may change from time to time and from situation to situation, depending on for example, one's age, to different stages in one's life, or to the rewards and incentives offered by the organisation.

For example, someone approaching retirement, which should place him at Maslow's level five, may be more concerned with satisfying his security needs related to his pension plan, which fall in level two. Many artists claim too that they have reached Maslow's final and highest level of self-actualisation without having their safety and belonging needs from the second and third lower levels, satisfied.

As the supervisor therefore you must consider at the end of the day that most people are motivated by, *"what's in it for me"* at that particular time in their lives. If you can recognise an individual's talents and skills and know what is important to him, in the now, you can use this to encourage and inspire him to excel.

This is easier said than done and exploring David McClelland's motivational theory, which uses Maslow's levels as the base will broaden our knowledge to learn how to better motivate our teams.

"It does not matter how slowly you go as long as you do not stop." - Confucius

Chapter 25

David McClelland's Human
Motivation Theory

"Motivation is a fire from within. If someone else tries to light that fire under you, chances are it will burn very briefly." - Stephen Covey

As a supervisor you have to remember that motivation is about boosting the confidence of your staff. They have to see their work resulting in some sort of reward for themselves. Each person, however, is driven by different individual needs and recognising this will help the supervisor to determine how to motivate each of them. In the early 1960's building on Maslow's theory, David McClelland identified three motivating drivers that we all have.

He stated that each of us has a combination of three main driving motivators namely; the need for *"achievement, affiliation and power".* These motivators are not inherent; we develop them through our culture and life experiences. As a result one of them thrives and becomes the dominant one which motivates us.

A person whose main, motivating driver is *"achievement"* wants the supervisor to recognise his input and give him feedback as he works. He actually has to also feel a personal sense of accomplishment. He will seek to attain realistic but challenging goals and advancement in the job. An achiever is ambitious and wants to climb the corporate ladder. He focuses on solving problems and meeting challenges. He also prefers to work alone. Can you identify anyone at your office with this motivating driver?

The second need is *"affiliation"* and someone with this as his prevailing driver wants friendly relationships and constant interaction with other people. He wants the supervisor and colleagues to like him. He would be a good team player who is always willing to help others. However, someone with a strong need for affiliation dislikes standing out or taking risks, he values relationships above anything else. He wants to feel like he belongs and would tend to agree with popular decisions despite his reservations. Does this describe any of your staff members?

Someone with the central motivating driver of *"power"* has a get-up-and-go attitude. He is determined to be influential, effective and to make an impact. He has a strong need to lead and for his ideas to prevail. He wants to be in charge and control others. He is willing to take risks and compete with others. He likes to win and wants public recognition when he does. Does this person sound familiar?

If you, as the supervisor, use this information to identify the motivating drivers of your team, it will then help you to get the best out of all of them. For instance, when delegating tasks, you are better able to choose the most suitable person. I can recall, when assigning work positions on board the aircraft, I considered the cabin crew member who had a strong achievement driver, to be responsible for the economy cabin service. This was because I knew that the service would be completed not only on time, but also, as was required by the airline.

It is equally important that you know your own principal driver since it will affect your behaviour and management style.

For example:
- ▼ A supervisor with a strong affiliation need would undermine his objectivity because he needs to be liked. This in turn would affect his decision making capability. It is okay to want to be liked, but as a supervisor it should not be the basis for your decisions. More than likely more problems, including interpersonal ones, will arise for him to manage.
- ▼ A supervisor with a strong power need would be attracted to a leadership role but he may not possess the required flexibility

and people-centered skills. Sometimes it is necessary to lead from the *"back"* and allow someone else to be in *"front"*. He would definitely have to guard against having too aggressive an attitude.

▼ A supervisor with a strong achievement need would make the best leader but there is a tendency to demand too much of his staff in the belief that they are like him, which of course they are not. Remember it is about maintaining the company's standards and not his own.

Which of the three is your dominant driver?

_____
_____
_____
_____
_____

"Desire is the key to motivation, but it's determination and commitment to an unrelenting pursuit of your goal — a commitment to excellence — that will enable you to attain the success you seek." - Mario Andretti

Chapter 26

"Know Thyself"

"Chance favours the prepared mind." - Louis Pasteur

The Greek proverb, *"know thyself"* is a useful recommendation that the supervisor can heed. It may surprise you to learn that how you see yourself and how others see you may not necessarily correspond. Be that as it may, if you have a clear and honest understanding of *"you"* then you are better able to manage yourself and others and in so doing, *"get the job done"* more efficiently. Additionally as *"chief cook and bottle-washer"* this knowledge will allow you to enhance your planning and organising skills. It helps in your decision making processes.

A personal *SWOT* analysis is a constructive technique that you can employ. *SWOT* is an acronym for:

S = *Strengths (internal)*

W = *Weaknesses (internal)*

O = *Opportunities (external)*

T = *Threats (external)*

It is a tool which will help you internally to identify your skills and recognise your weaknesses so that they don't affect the job you do. It also helps you to see external opportunities that you may not realise are there. Knowing your weaknesses helps you to remove/reduce external threats that can hinder your progress. In other words, this information will help you to bridge the gap from where you are to where you want to be. Here is a simple example;

Strengths	Weaknesses
▼ Your technical skills ▼ Patience ▼ Communication skills ▼ Fairness	▼ Lack of technical skills ▼ Delegation ▼ Time management ▼ Sense of humor
Opportunities	Threats
▼ Technical skills courses ▼ Promotion ▼ Company's expanding	▼ Failing technical courses ▼ New competition ▼ Changes in technologies

A **SWOT** analysis is a big picture.

Internally:

Having identified your strengths you can now decide how you can best use them. You will also be able to recognise your weaknesses and learn how to remove or overcome them.

Externally:

You will be able to source opportunities to grow. You will also identify the threats that are in the way of your success so that you can conquer them.

For example, when I decided to clip my wings and become a training officer, this tool helped me to put things in perspective. I had to identify the specific training this entailed (the opportunity). Then I had to re-organise my lifestyle, despite the time and other constraints (the threats) to succeed. This was easier said than done, but armed with determination and perseverance, I did it!

In conducting your personal swot analysis, it is important to be honest, objective and realistic. Specifically distinguish where you are today and where you can be tomorrow. In relation to the competition, bench mark your skills and knowledge. Also don't be too hard on yourself, keep it simple and straight-forward. You will then be able to take action to make the changes you desire.

Why not start practicing now? Complete your personal SWOT analysis below.

Strengths	Weaknesses
Opportunities	Threats

A swot analysis can also be used to identify your team's strengths. You will then be able to acknowledge their expertise, knowledge and skills and as a result be better able to decide how to sustain and develop them. Also being able to identify their weaknesses will allow you to choose the best course of action to address them. Searching for available opportunities will encourage you to think outside the box in looking for new ways to improve and further develop your team. Obviously the threats can be removed or mitigated once they have been identified.

Remember by providing training, by motivating, and by recognising the team's achievements you can bridge the gap from where they are to where you want them all to be.

"Man often becomes what he believes himself to be. If I keep on saying to myself that I cannot do a certain thing, it is possible that I may end by really becoming incapable of doing it. On the contrary, if I have the belief that I can do it, I shall surely acquire the capacity to do it even if I may not have it at the beginning." - Mahatma Gandhi

Chapter 27

Conclusion

Conclusion

"Success consists of doing the common things of life uncommonly well." - Unknown

There are many tools available to help the supervisor develop. By now though you will have a good understanding of how to:

▼ Define the supervisor and characterise supervision
▼ Acknowledge the supervisor's responsibilities including his managerial duties
▼ Identify some of the main challenges/problems he may encounter
▼ Ascertain how he can enhance his expertise though improved:
  - Interpersonal relationships
  - Communication
  - Time management
  - Leadership
  - Motivational and support skills

You see, despite being a junior manager, the supervisor/superhero can embrace success and in time even become the managing director/CEO of an organisation. I agree that because of his present status position he is caught between a rock and a hard place. However, there is absolutely no need for him to stay there. Like Superman, he is gifted with the ability to lead his team to victory and in so doing climb the corporate ladder of success.

Remember, even then, he will still be planning, organising, leading and controlling. It is his scope and focus that changes. So enjoy being a superhero and continue to hone your skills. There is nothing to stop you from being a great leader even if you are the most junior manager. I found this lovely poem by Meiji Stewart which is a super way to end this book. If you read it every day you will consistently remind yourself of the important role you play as a supervisor.

Great Leaders...
Awaken minds.
Bring people together.
Communicate effectively.
Dare to take calculated risks.
Enlighten and empower.
Foster collaboration.
Give you tools to succeed.
Help you do for yourself.
Invite and encourage questions.
Joyfully embrace diversity.
Keep an open mind.
Lead by example.
Motivate with respect.
Never give up on you.
Open doors to new worlds.
Put first things first.
Quest to make learning fun.
Recognise problems early.
Share roles and responsibilities.
Take time to explain things.
Unwrap talents and abilities.
Value everyone's input.
Welcome mistakes as part of learning.
Xceed expectations.
Yearn to connect, not correct.
Zest to make a difference.
© Meiji Stewart.

Conclusion

"A mediocre person tells. A good person explains. A superior person demonstrates. A great person inspires others to see for themselves."
- Harvey Mackay

Index

Symbols
80/20 rule 68, 70, 71, 72
80/20 theory 71

A
abilities XII, XIII, 12, 19, 47, 50, 110
Abraham Lincoln 11, 68
Abraham Maslow 96
A Theory of Human Motivation V, 95, 96, 97
Accomplish more in less time 72
achievement 16, 100, 101, 102
Achievement 93
acronym 104
act 2, 11, 16, 20, 22, 43, 53, 54, 59, 62, 90, 94
a daily basis 71, 72
administer 2
Adolph Hitler 81
adopted XII
advertisements 72
advice 3, 39, 67, 68
affiliation 100, 101
Aggressive 52, 54
aircraft 3, 11, 16, 20, 30, 32, 45, 53, 58, 82, 101
airline XIV, 3, 6, 7, 25, 82, 101
Alonso, "The Quiet Profession" 8
America 3
Anthea Turner 74

Anthony Robbins 52
apply XII, XIII, 11, 71
appreciated 39
approve 26, 94
aspiration 81
Assertive 52, 53
A Theory of Human Motivation V, 95, 96, 97
attitude XII, 12, 32, 101, 102
attributes XII, 20
authority 20, 21, 22, 32, 74, 78, 81, 87

B

bad 17, 81
Barriers 47
behaviours 54, 89
Be kind and considerate 22
Benjamin Disraeli 6
best practices 12
Be trustworthy 22
Bill Bradley 85
Billy Shall 71, 72
blueprint 15
body language 43, 49
Bottom line 94
Brian Tracy 56
budget restrictions 19
build XIII, 10, 26, 44, 48, 55, 75, 78, 79
building rapport 26

build morale 78

Business XII, 38

Byron Dorgan 78

C

cabin attendant 6

cabin crew 7, 11, 19, 32, 101

Cabin crew 7

CEO 11, 71, 109

chains of command 10

challenges XIII, XIV, 7, 24, 25, 100, 109

challenges/problems XIII, XIV, 109

challenge the process 90

challenging 6, 27, 40, 55, 58, 100

character 81

characteristics XIII, 20

character traits 81

charitable social agencies 3

checked flights 32

chief cook and bottle-washer 104

classes 26

clear-cut goals 6

clock time 66, 67

"clock time and real time" 66

"Clock Time and Real Time" V, 65, 67

close friends 71

cloud the interaction 47

collective agreements 19

commitment 11, 36, 74, 78, 87, 102

Commitment to staff 12

communication XIII, 40, 43, 44, 45, 47, 48, 49, 50, 52, 53

Communication V, XIV, 24, 42, 43, 44, 45, 46, 47, 49, 50, 51, 53, 55, 56, 105, 109

communication skills 40, 43, 45, 50

Communication skills 105

Communication Style V, 51, 53, 55

company 3, 7, 11, 12, 19, 20, 21, 25, 32, 40, 86, 87, 102

company's policies 12

competent XIII, 79

compliance 32

compromising 39

Conclusion V, 108, 109, 111

confidence 26, 33, 36, 38, 39, 75, 78, 86, 87, 100

conflicts 39

Confucius 24, 98

consultant XII

control 2, 20, 29, 33, 59, 60, 62, 63, 101

controller 3

controlling 10, 14, 17, 59, 62, 63, 109

cost 12, 21

CEO Logic 71

C. Ray Johnson 71

credit VIII, XII, 50, 94

crisis situations 78

criticise 33

D

Dan Millman 70

David McClelland V, 98, 99, 100, 101

David McClelland's Human Motivation Theory 99

default 52, 53, 55

defeat 7

Define the supervisor and characterise supervision XIV, 109

definition XI, 2, 43, 59, 66, 70, 81

definitions 43, 62

Delano and Shah 2007 XIII

delegating 12, 17, 79, 101

Delegation V, 24, 73, 74, 75, 77, 79, 105

Delegation Tips V, 77, 79

de-motivators 93

Denis Waitley 50

department 3, 7, 22, 32, 82

designed XIII, 14, 66

details/message 44

determination 81, 90, 102, 105

Develop 75

Developing Interpersonal Relationship Skills 37

difficult people 33

direct 2, 53

director/CEO 109

disciplinary actions 78

discipline 8, 12

Distance 94

duties XIV, 6, 10, 11, 12, 40, 74, 109

Dwight Eisenhower 94

dynamic XIII, 82

E

earn 7, 38

Earth XIV

effectively communicate 47, 52

Eliminate information overload 72

Eliminate stress 71

Elisabeth Foley 30

emails 72

embrace success through skillful supervision XIII

Embracing Success I, III, IV, VII, 58

Embracing Success through Time Management 58

emotional intelligence 24, 41

Emotional Intelligence 89

emotions 47

Empathise 22

employ 3, 74, 104

employee of the month 97

enable others to act 90

encourage XIV, 3, 36, 40, 50, 83, 90, 98, 107, 110

Environment 94

Epicurus 27

etiquette 38

Europe 3

Evaluates 12

executive director 10, 11

Exercise: 85

expenditure 12

Experience 21

Explain and listen 22

external auditor 26

Externally 105

F

facilitated 26, 82

fair 16, 39, 97

familiarity breeds contempt 6

family IX, XII, 3, 60, 71, 97

faster 47, 71, 76, 79

fault 39

feelings 38, 43, 53, 54

Financial reward 93

fine-tune 22

First Officer 11

flight attendants 26

Flight Engineer 11

foreman 3

For example 14, 16, 17, 20, 47, 50, 62, 66, 75, 78, 89, 97, 101, 105

four communication goals 44

four main functions 14

friends IX, 29, 30, 39, 60, 62, 71, 96

friends and peers 29

Fully delegate 75

Functions of Management V, 13, 15, 17

future trends 11

G

general workers 6, 11

Geoffrey Chaucer 58

George S. Patton 79

gets his hands dirty 6

get the job done 91, 104

goals 2, 6, 12, 15, 17, 44, 48, 64, 96, 100

goals, results, and objectives 15

good VII, 4, 12, 16, 24, 25, 26, 30, 36, 39, 53, 66, 67, 81, 87, 89, 90, 91, 101, 109, 111

good judgment 39

Good working atmosphere 93

great leaders 20, 89

Greta Scacchi 36

grow XII, 30, 75, 105

H

habits 12

handle 2, 7, 60

Harvey Mackay 111

Hawkins and Shohet 2

Hazy job profile 94

healthier life styles 3

Helping others 93

Henry Mintzberg 17

Henry Winkler 43

hero VIII, XII, XIII, 14

H - Have patience 40

hierarchical 32

hierarchical structure 32

hierarchy 94, 96, 97

Historical Background 3

honest VIII, 39, 48, 53, 104, 106

honest serving men 48

"How" 15, 49

human XII, XIV, 47

Human Motivation V, 95, 96, 97, 101

hypothesis 71

I

"importance" 63, 67

important activities 71

improve XIII, 12, 16, 22, 33, 36, 38, 44, 45, 47, 48, 50, 52, 55, 56, 59, 60, 71, 89, 97, 107

Improve relationships 71

Improving your Communication Skills V, 46

In a nutshell 71, 91

inappropriately 38

in-charge 19, 32

in-charge cabin crew member (purser) 32

increase production 12, 39

incredible XII

individual 7, 11, 12, 35, 50, 52, 81, 82, 93, 98, 100

individual goals 12

in-flight 3, 17, 82

information IV, 21, 22, 35, 38, 43, 44, 47, 48, 55, 72, 101, 105

Information 21

information consumption 72

inspire 50, 83, 90, 91, 98

inspire a shared vision 90

Internally 105

interpersonal XIII, 24, 25, 33, 35, 36, 38, 40, 101

Interpersonal relationships XIV, 24, 109

Interpersonal skills 24

J

Jago 81

James William 32

Jimmy Dean 22

job XII, 2, 3, 6, 7, 11, 16, 21, 25, 58, 82, 90, 91, 94, 97, 100, 104, 105

John Maxwell 82

John Powell 45

Joy Kelshall III, IV, VII

judgment 35, 39

junior manager 10, 109, 110

K

Keep an open mind 22, 110

Kelshall III, IV, VII

Ken Blanchard 89

Kenneth Blanchard 81

know how 16, 25, 38

Knowing your Communication Style V, 51

knowledge 21, 22, 25, 26, 75, 81, 90, 98, 104, 106, 107

knowledge and skills 25, 81, 107

Know Thyself V, 103, 105, 107

L

lack of interest 40, 47, 75

leader 3, 16, 36, 81, 87, 91, 102, 109

leader/manager 91

leaders 20, 81, 82, 87, 89, 90, 91

leadership XIII, 22, 44, 81, 82, 83, 85, 87, 89, 93, 101

Leadership V, XIV, 24, 80, 81, 83, 84, 85, 86, 87, 88, 89, 91, 109

leadership capabilities 89

Leadership/Leaders 86

leadership models 89

Leadership Models V, 88, 89, 91

leadership situations 22

Leadership versus Management V, 84, 85, 87

Leadership vs Management 86

leading 10, 14, 16, 87, 91, 93, 109

Lee Iacocca 10, 16

Level Five Leadership 89

licensing restrictions 19

life styles 3

listened 47

listening abilities 47

listening skills training 47

Lose weight 72

Louis Pasteur 104

Lucius Annaeus Seneca 29

M

made and not born 81, 91

Mahatma Gandhi 20, 107

Manage 26, 35, 75

Management/Managers 86

management process 14

manager XII

managerial duties XIV, 109

managerial responsibilities 6

manager's XII

mandatory safety training 26, 32

Manipulative 52, 55

map 15

Mario Andretti 102

Mark Millar XIV

Martin Luther King, Jr. 91

Maslow's levels 96, 98

Meiji Stewart 110

member 16, 19, 32, 35, 75, 79, 101

merit 7

Micromanagement 94

micromanaging 78

middle managers 10, 11

Mike Murdock 38

mind clutter 47

model the way 90

morale 78, 93

motivate 36, 78, 83, 91, 93, 94, 97, 98, 100

motivates 93, 100

motivates people 93

motivating drivers 100, 101

motivational XIII, 94, 98

Motivational and support skills XIV, 109

Motivation and Support V, 92, 93

Ms. Newton 53, 54, 55

N

Nancy Kline 4

Needs of belonging 96

Nelson Mandela 81

news 44, 53, 66, 72

noise 47, 49

Nonito Donaire 96

No recognition 94

North America 3

O

objectives 11, 12, 15, 17, 71, 79, 87

observe 2, 26, 38

official 3

one's development 89

O - Optimistic 39

operating 6

Opportunities 104, 105, 106

organisation VIII, IX, XII, 6, 10, 11, 39, 40, 87, 90, 97, 109

Organisational support 12

organise 2, 14, 15, 16, 70, 81, 105

organising 10, 14, 15, 79, 104, 109

outside the box 39, 107

overburden 76

overload 72

oversee 2

overworked 76

P

Pareto Principle 70, 71

Pareto's Principle 68, 70, 72

participation XIV

Passive-aggressive 52

Paul Hawken 14

Paul Hersey 89

Paul J. Meyer 47

peers 29, 97

people VI, XI, XII, XIII, XIV, 2, 3, 6, 10, 16, 20, 22, 24, 25, 33, 41, 44, 47, 50, 53, 54, 55, 63, 70, 74, 75, 79, 83, 85, 86, 87, 89, 93, 94, 96, 98, 101, 102, 110

people skills VI, 24, 41

People Skills 24

perform XII, 10, 12, 16, 36

performance 2, 7, 17, 19, 35, 40

performances 12

performance skills 19

permission IV, 19, 54, 81

person VIII, XII, 2, 3, 7, 20, 21, 35, 40, 41, 44, 47, 48, 62, 74, 79, 81, 82, 100, 101, 111

Personal 63

personal best 89

personal qualities 20, 22

personal time 78

Peter F. Drucker 60

phases 14

Physical environment 93

Physiological needs 96

pilots 26

plan 11, 14, 15, 17, 35, 36, 58, 63, 67, 78, 97, 98

Planning 14, 15

"planning and preparation" 63

"planning, prioritising and controlling" 63

Plato 25

playing field 7

policies 11, 12, 19

Policies 94

polite 38

Politics 94

position XIII, 6, 20, 21, 32, 33, 38, 49, 81, 86, 109

positive work attitude 12

possessions 71

power XIV, 19, 20, 21, 22, 54, 81, 100, 101

practice 7, 17, 30, 55
preserve 29
prime minister 20
prioritise 71
Prioritising with the 80/20 Rule V, 69, 71
privileges 10
problems XIII, XIV, 14, 17, 36, 71, 79, 86, 93, 100, 101, 109, 110
procedure 6
produce IX, 60, 67, 71, 72
Professional 64
professional relationships 29
profitability IX, XIII
promote 6
promoted 7, 82, 97
protocol 38
Proverbs 29:18 83
Purge the clutter 71
purpose XIII, 48, 78
Purser 3, 6, 11
putting out fires 26
pyramid 96, 97

Q

quality XIII, 7, 12, 21, 56, 71
quantity 12

R

Rainer Maria Rilke 41

real management XI, XII

Recognition 93

Redeploy 75

regulations 12, 87

relationships XIII, XIV, 24, 25, 27, 29, 33, 35, 36, 38, 39, 40, 43, 44, 50, 55, 71, 100, 101, 109

respect XII, 7, 20, 33, 38, 54, 79, 87, 90, 110

responsibilities XIII, XIV, 6, 10, 11, 12, 19, 20, 22, 36, 109, 110

results 6, 14, 15, 17, 36, 49, 54, 58, 63, 67, 71, 72, 75, 79, 89

rise to the bait 33

risk 12

R - Respect 38

R - Restore confidence 39

Rudyard Kipling's poem 48

run 2

Russell H. Ewin 87

S

safe environment 12

Safety needs 96

safety training 26, 32

Salary 94

Sam Walton 89

saving time 72, 78

Self-actualisation 96

self-confidence 33

Self-esteem 96

self-sufficient 3

senior 6, 10, 21, 26, 32

senior managers 10, 21

Sense of humor 105

Servant Leadership 89

serve two masters 6

side-by-side 6

Situational Leadership 89

skill 50, 56, 74

Skillful Supervision I, III, VII

skills VI, VII, VIII, XIII, XIV, 6, 12, 19, 22, 24, 25, 36, 38, 40, 41, 43, 44, 45, 47, 50, 52, 59, 60, 63, 74, 75, 78, 81, 90, 91, 96, 97, 98, 102, 104, 105, 106, 107, 109

snapshot 3

social 3, 36, 60, 67

soft skills 24, 41

Solving problems 93

special 39

specific tasks 16, 81

spouse 71

S - Support 39

staff IX, 6, 10, 11, 12, 25, 39, 40, 47, 76, 78, 79, 87, 90, 97, 100, 101, 102

staff capabilities 78

stage 6

status 20, 29, 86, 109

steadfast 81

steadfast determination 81

Stephen Covey 33, 66, 72, 79, 100

stimulate 93

strengths 16, 22, 63, 71, 105, 107

Strengths 104, 105, 106

strengths and weaknesses 16, 22, 71

stress 55, 71

Submissive 52, 54

succeed 10, 30, 36, 41, 58, 67, 87, 105, 110

successful leader 81

succession 78

succession plan 78

success or failure 74

super VIII, XII, XIII, 3, 14, 15, 26, 90, 110

super-human XII

superintend 2

superintendent 3

Superman XII, XIV, 14, 19, 35, 109

supervision XII

supervisor XII

supervisors VII, XII, 3, 7, 10, 11, 24, 32, 75, 78

supervisor's responsibilities XIV, 109

Supervisor's Trials V, 23, 25, 27

supervisor/superhero 109

SWOT 104, 105, 106

SWOT analysis 104, 105, 106

Systems of Time Management V, 61, 63

T

take charge of 2

Talents 19, 21

Talents power 21

task 2, 6, 16, 29, 59, 67, 74, 75, 76, 79, 82

team 3, 7, 11, 16, 17, 26, 35, 36, 38, 39, 50, 52, 74, 75, 78, 79, 81, 87, 90, 91, 94, 97, 101, 107, 109

team leader 3

team spirit 78

teamwork 12

technical courses 105

technical skills 6, 24, 105

tenure XIV, 11

The Aggressive Style 54

The Assertive Style 53

The communication process 44

The Five Practices of Exemplary Leadership® Model 89

The Manipulative Style 55

The Passive Aggressive Style 54

The Role of the Supervisor/ Manager in Interpersonal Relationships 34

The Submissive Style 54

The Supervisor V, 5, 7, 23, 25, 27

The Vocation of the Supervisor V, 9, 11

"Things to do list" 62

Think before you act 22

Threats 104, 105, 106

time VIII, XIII, 3, 7, 15, 16, 17, 26, 29, 30, 32, 35, 36, 38, 47, 49, 54, 55, 58, 59, 60, 62, 63, 64, 66, 67, 68, 70, 71, 72, 76, 78, 79, 87, 94, 97, 98,

101, 105, 109, 110

timely 12

timely manner 12

time management XIII, 58, 59, 60, 62, 63, 64, 70, 71, 72

Time Management IV, V, 57, 58, 59, 61, 63

Timings 94

Title 19, 20

Title power 20

To build relationships 44

to encourage the heart 90

To inform 44

To persuade 44

To request 44

training 21, 26, 32, 40, 47, 58, 64, 75, 81, 82, 94, 105, 107

Training 21

training session 26, 58

training supervisors 32

traits 20, 81

Traits 19, 22

Traits power 22

Trial #1 23, 25

Trial # 2 V, 28, 29

Trial #3 V, 31

trivial activities 71, 72

trusting 29

trustworthy 22, 38

T - Talk & listen 40

T - Thank 39

T - Trust 38

two masters 6, 11, 12, 58

two-way process 44, 49

U

unbiased 39

United States of America 3

Unknown 19, 76, 109

unprofessional 38

Unrealistic workload 94

unsuccessful 7

usurp 32

U - Understand 39

V

Value 38, 110

Varied & interesting work 93

vehicle XIII

vision XII, XIV, 11, 12, 15, 82, 83, 86, 87, 90

vision & policies 12

W

watch 2, 3

watch and observe 2

Wayne Dyer 35

weaknesses 16, 22, 55, 63, 71, 105, 107

Weaknesses 104, 105, 106

"What" 15, 48

What is Supervision V, 1, 3

What's In It For Me 94

"When" 15, 49

"Where" 15, 49

"Who" 15, 50

"Why" 15, 48

WIIFM 94

William Penn 64

willingness 74

Winston Churchill 62

work VII, IX, XI, XII, XIII, 2, 3, 6, 7, 11, 12, 14, 15, 16, 25, 29, 30, 35, 36, 39, 45, 56, 60, 62, 66, 67, 71, 72, 74, 75, 78, 79, 81, 87, 90, 93, 94, 96, 97, 100, 101

workers 3, 6, 7, 11, 12, 32, 36, 38, 39, 40

working relationship 29

working smart 72

Working with others 93

W - Wisdom 39

Y

years of service 6

Y - The yardstick 40

www.ingramcontent.com/pod-product-compliance
Lightning Source LLC
Chambersburg PA
CBHW042336040426
42446CB00021B/3473